IMPORTANT

YOU MUST READ THE FOLLOWING BEFORE CONTINUING

In a recent international survey, more than 63% of people believed that within the next decade the world would be facing a zombie apocalypse – when the shuffling dead emerge in such numbers that our civilisation is simply overwhelmed.

However, all is not lost. You hold in your hands one of the most comprehensive survival manuals ever produced. Richly illustrated and packed with the latest scientific updates, it will take you through everything you need to know to stay alive when the rest of the world is being feasted upon. From what a zombie is and where they come from, to how to kill them and develop your own survival plan, it's all in this volume, which I hope will become a well-used guide as you prepare to face the walking dead. This book is designed to educate, train, amuse, scare and prepare, and not always in that order.

If you currently consider yourself an 'unbeliever', welcome also and read on. For within these pages you'll find detailed and documented evidence of zombie outbreaks through history as well as corroborated scientific proof that the zombie virus and zombies exist. We are fortunate to have had exclusive access to the scientist many consider to be the founding father of zombiology, Dr Khalid Ahmed.

But, don't worry, this isn't just a text book. There's a stack of information on innovative ways to take out zombies and some downright dangerous advice on everything from creating a zombie-busting wheelchair to building devastating traps to ensnare the walking dead.

And, at the back, there is a chance to test your knowledge and become a certified zombie survivalist. Now that will be something to tell them about at school or add to your CV.

If you've been scared by zombie films, been kept up at night by zombie books, or just have an unhealthy fear that the world is about to end, and that zombies will most certainly have a role in it, then this is the book for you.

Finally, don't be ashamed that you are only now learning about zombies. Read this book in public, let folks see you are concerned about the dead. You'll be surprised how many will tap you on the shoulder and say 'hey, I'm worried about zombies too'. It can be a real eye-opener and a great way to make some unusual new friends.

By picking up this Haynes manual you've taken the first step to saying 'I will survive the zombies', so read on, make notes in the margins, scribble things on bits of paper and start making your own plans. Things are about to get very strange.

Sean T. Page
Ministry of Zombies, London

CONTENTS

WHAT IS A ZOMBIE?

Before beginning any reading or course in zombie survival, it is essential that you have a clear understanding of what a zombie is, how it is created, the main types and, most important of all, how you can 'kill' a zombie.

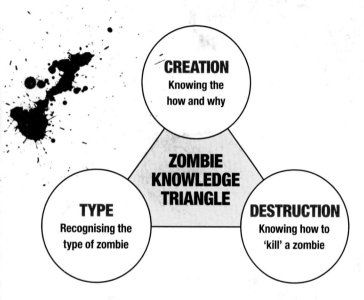

ZOMBIE KNOWLEDGE TRIANGLE

CREATION Knowing the how and why

TYPE Recognising the type of zombie

DESTRUCTION Knowing how to 'kill' a zombie

These three factors are the foundation of any zombie survival plan and are referred to as the Zombie Knowledge Triangle. All zombie survivalists must clearly understand how a zombie is created, be able to recognise the different types and deal with the walking dead.

> **A ZOMBIE IS A DEAD BODY THAT HAS BEEN BROUGHT BACK TO ANIMATION BY A COMPLEX RNA VIRUS WHICH LEADS THE BODY TO BEHAVE IN A CANNIBALISTIC WAY**
>
> **MINISTRY OF ZOMBIES HANDBOOK**

To be clear, the zombic condition, which is characterised by the slow stagger, lumbering walk and violent appetite for the flesh of the living, are all classic symptoms of the zombie virus. So, there is nothing supernatural, nothing spooky and nothing superhuman about the walking dead. They are simply humans transformed into very different creatures. But always remember that once a human has become infected with the virus, typically by a bite from an infected zombie, then the transformation will begin. More detail is given on this process further in this volume but know this:

THERE IS CURRENTLY NO CURE FOR THE ZOMBIE VIRUS AND ONCE CONTRACTED BY A HUMAN, TRANSFORMATION INTO A ZOMBIE IS A CERTAINTY

WHAT IS A ZOMBIE?
ZOMBIE CREATION MYTHS

In a recent survey by GeoPol, fewer than 23% of Americans realised that zombism is caused by a virus. Here is a breakdown that shows the level of misunderstanding among the public of the root cause of zombies.

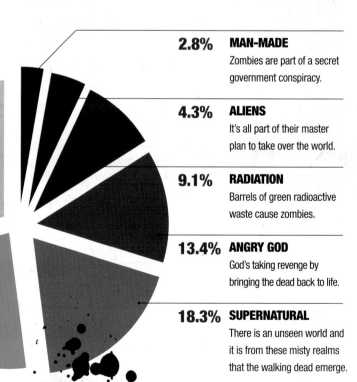

2.8% MAN-MADE
Zombies are part of a secret government conspiracy.

4.3% ALIENS
It's all part of their master plan to take over the world.

9.1% RADIATION
Barrels of green radioactive waste cause zombies.

13.4% ANGRY GOD
God's taking revenge by bringing the dead back to life.

18.3% SUPERNATURAL
There is an unseen world and it is from these misty realms that the walking dead emerge.

29.3% VOODOO
Magic, myth and the poison from the rare puffer fish leads to mindless undead slaves.

22.8% VIRUS
The world of science has the answer – it's caused by a virus.

SURVEY OF 1028 PEOPLE IN NEW YORK IN DECEMBER 2012

MINISTRY OF ZOMBIES

► HOW TO SPOT A ZOMBIE

KNOW THE SIGNS!

Scruffy Bohemian student or 'back from the office late' drunk may each display signs of the zombic condition, but it doesn't necessarily mean you should run and get the axe. It is vital that you clearly identify your target as a zombie before you get chopping. Be on the lookout for the following:

► A vacant and distant gaze, which only becomes agitated at the prospect of living flesh. The creature will emit a low-level guttural groan.

► A pallid, deathly colourless skin. Eyes may be milky or tinged with red. Both nails and hair may have grown giving the figure a distinctive 'hippie' look and smell.

► Clothes may be ripped or torn. There may be obvious injuries such as clear bite marks or missing limbs, but equally there may be no visible signs of trauma or dried blood.

► Slow, stumbling walk. Zombies appear unbalanced and awkward, often tripping and falling over minor obstacles. Newly converted zombies will display a better level of movement and dexterity.

► The walking dead will always move towards the living with the express purpose of turning them into their next meat snack.

BE WARNED CITIZENS!

WHAT IS A ZOMBIE?

TYPES OF ZOMBIE

Once a human has turned into a zombie, they will enter a three-stage process of transformation. All will go through these stages, but factors such as climate, body mass and the amount of infected material will have an impact.

To be clear, these are not stages of the 'illness' – these will be reviewed later. For now, these humans have already transformed into the undead, they are fully infected with zombie virus and display symptoms of the zombic condition. In 2008, Dr Ahmed shocked the zombie-fighting community when he declared that 'all zombies are not equal.' He later went on to expand on a scientific theory of zombie evolution, which describes how the undead develop over the course of time after infection. For many years, survivalists had offered accounts of desiccated zombies or huge bloated corpse-monsters, but the fledging science of Zombiology had no unified theory to explain these anomalies. Dr Ahmed's stages of zombie evolution changed all of this and they are presented below.

▶ ZOMBIE EVOLUTION

◀ **STAGE 1**
FRESH
(NOOBS, NEWBIES, INHUMOS)

These walking dead have contracted the zombie virus in the last few days. They have a pallid, grey/blue skin colour and a bloodless complexion. Some will appear almost human in appearance; others will be missing major body parts. Importantly, their movements will be stiff and awkward, they will be unable to speak and they will have an unhealthy interest in feasting on your flesh.

▶ **STAGE 2**
PUTREFIED
(SICKIES, PUKERS, FATTIES, BUG BOYS, BLOATERS)

At this stage, zombies generally start to show signs of decomposition. For example, you may see pus-filled wounds and green fungus patches appearing. However, the decomposition process is greatly decelerated by the zombic condition. In humid conditions, excess acid or gastric liquid may swell the corpse to an enormous size.

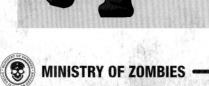

WHAT IS A ZOMBIE?

CLIMATIC CONDITIONS

Experiments have now proved that it is climatic conditions which have the greatest influence on the 'type' of creature that survivors will face after Z-Day. For example, fighters in hot and humid, tropical or sub-tropical climates are likely to face more putrefied and bloated zombies whereas fighters in arid and desert conditions will battle dried and skeletal ghouls.

■ TUNDRA
■ TEMPERATE
▨ DESERT
░ TROPICAL

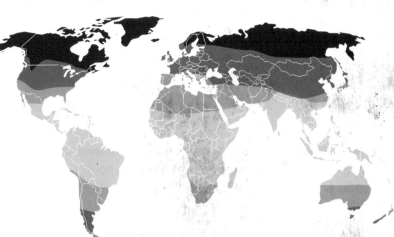

▶ **STAGE 3**
DESICCATED
(CLASSICS, ZEDS, STIFFS, STENCHIES, HIPPIES)

Most of the walking dead will move into this 'classic' zombie phase of development. These creatures will be barely human in appearance. Their skin will be thin and stretched; their wounds dry and cracked. By this stage, their clothes will be mostly tattered and their eyes turned a milky shade, even yellowish in some cases. Climatic conditions will determine the actual level of moisture in a classic zombie, with dry conditions leading to a skeletal creature on which the skin hangs like a rotting, almost transparent blanket. Over time, injury or rotten body parts may just fall off with the creature seemingly oblivious to any loss.

ONCE INFECTED BY BITE OR FLUID EXCHANGE, A HUMAN WILL TRANSFORM INTO A ZOMBIE AND MOVE THROUGH THESE ZOMBIE TYPES

TROPICAL High temperature, high humidity

Bloated masses of dead flesh in addition to a veritable explosion in the insect life and fungus surrounding these walking corpses.

▶ High numbers of 'bloaters'.
▶ Higher rate of decomposition.
▶ More fungal growth.

DESERT High temperature, low humidity

Often referred to as 'skeleton corpses', the dead will be thin and wiry with more exposed bone than in other regions.

▶ Parched zombies.
▶ Skeletal husks.
▶ Bleached flesh stretched tightly.

TEMPERATE Low temperature, high humidity

Survivors should prepare to face all types of zombie in the initial outbreak. Depending on the season, most will move towards the classic phase.

▶ Most zombies will be at the desiccated stage within a month.
▶ Fewer bloaters than the tropics.

TUNDRA Low temperature, low humidity

Winter will often keep the dead fully frozen and easy to deal with, but the thaw can see zombies emerge in a particularly rotten and hungry mood.

▶ Zombies may be frozen solid and dormant.
▶ Very low level of decomposition.

WHAT IS A ZOMBIE?

HOW TO KILL A ZOMBIE ——

Weapons and more advanced unarmed combat techniques that can be used against the dead will be discussed later. For now it's enough to know that to kill a zombie you must destroy at least 80% of its brain. Nothing else will work. In zombie combat, we define 'killing' a zombie as meaning removing it as threat – in other words, taking it out of the game by ensuring that it never gets up. Technically speaking, you can't 'kill' what's already dead, but destroying a high proportion of a zombie's brain will prevent the creature rising again and seeking to feast on the flesh of the living.

A BLOW WHICH DOES NOT CONNECT SQUARELY WITH THE ZOMBIE SKULL WILL NOT DO ENOUGH DAMAGE SO PRACTISE YOUR ACCURACY

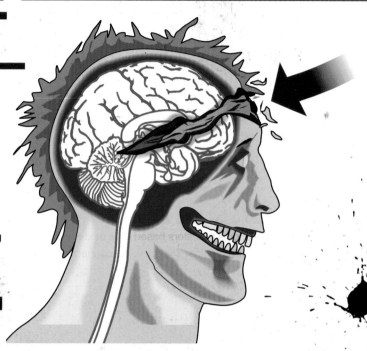

▶ A TYPICAL THREE-STEP PROCEDURE

STEP 1
IDENTIFY THE ZOMBIE

Recognise the creature, shout a warning if you can, then get prepared for action! Remember, the zombie in front of you is no longer human so act with purpose. Do not endanger yourself with any warning; there may be occasions when you need to move quickly through Step 1.

STEP 2
HEAD BASH OR KNOCK DOWN

If you have a weapon, go for a solid club to the head. Aim for the top of the skull and use force but be accurate – a glancing blow may not do the trick. If you are unarmed, you will need to sweep the creature's legs or kick it down. Remember, only a solid blow to the head will knock the creature down for good.

WHAT IS A ZOMBIE? COMMON MISCONCEPTIONS

More than any creature, the zombie is surrounded by legend, myth and misinformation. The zombie survivalist needs to be aware of these misconceptions. During the zombie apocalypse, panic and lies will be everywhere, rumours of their superpowers will be rife, and such tales will haunt the dreams of any survivors.

AREN'T THEY JUST LIKE VAMPIRES?

Vampires are fictional monsters based on a mixture of folklore and creative writing. They have no connection to zombies. There is nothing sparkly or romantic about 'the undead' and you won't be joining 'Team Edward' or 'Team Jacob' when the dead rise. You're more likely to be driving an axe through his skull than losing yourself in his good looks.

SHOULD I STAY AWAY FROM CEMETERIES?

For the seasoned zombie fighter, a cemetery should hold none of the horror it seems to for fans of ghost or vampire stories. It is a virus which causes the zombic condition. There is nothing supernatural about it and, statistically, very few zombies 'rise from the grave'. The incubation period for the virus means that there are far more outbreaks in hospital morgues than in chapels of rest or graveyards.

DON'T ZOMBIES JUST EAT BRAINS?

The most powerful myth surrounding zombies is that they only eat brains. Indeed, the classic "Brraaaaiinnss!" catchphrase supposedly muttered by the dead could seriously mislead survivors. Firstly, zombies will happily eat any part of a living or very recently deceased human. Secondly, zombies cannot talk.

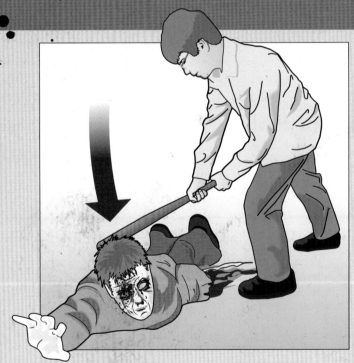

STEP 3
SECOND BLOW OR STAMP

Zombies are extremely robust creatures, so always be sure by delivering a second blow. Never assume that your one hit has done the job. Many an experienced zombie fighter has been bitten on the lower leg by a ghoul they thought they'd dealt with. For once, the movies got it right – always use the double-tap rule.

IF THEY ARE FRIENDS OR FAMILY, SURELY THEY'LL KNOW WHO I AM?

Simple answer, no! Once a human has transformed into a zombie, they have virtually no recollection of their former life. They are no longer the person they once were. So if zombie grandma staggers into view, it won't be to drop off any last-minute birthday or Christmas presents. Do not be deceived by the physical resemblance to your loved one. It's time to get busy with the axe. The zombic condition completely transforms any human into a ravenous and cannibalistic creature, and scientific experiments have shown that zombies will attack and feast upon the living, no matter who they are. It may not be easy driving a weapon into your neighbour's face or bashing a friend in with a baseball bat, so if necessary get someone else to do it. But, be assured, if you don't deal with zombie grandma, she will come drooling at the window. Finally, never attempt to bring a relative with the zombic condition into your fortified home. Where a member of your party has become infected, you should isolate them and then deal with them when they turn if you can't do it beforehand.

ANY BLOW TO A ZOMBIE HEAD WILL RESULT IN INFECTED BRAIN SPLATTER. BE ALERT TO THE RISK OF INFECTION

THE SCIENCE OF ZOMBIOLOGY

The fledgling science of zombiology is the study of both the zombie virus itself and the associated zombic condition it causes in humans. Although still largely discounted by mainstream academics, more and more research is being conducted into this area.

After an intensive period of field work in northwest India between 1997 and 2001, it was microbiologist and anthropologist Dr Khalid Ahmed who first isolated the complex RNA virus that triggers the development of the zombic condition. He became the first to fully document the virus and the remarkably metamorphosing effect it has on the human brain and body.

Since 2002, Dr Ahmed's research has been supported and developed by institutions and individuals around the world, but there are still many unanswered questions in the science of zombiology. For example, the biology behind certain zombie types such as the 'snapper', which is an infected head that has been separated from the body and yet continues to live and try to consume human flesh. However, the single greatest obstacle to scientific progress in the field of zombiology is the opposition and downright hostility of the world's universities and the research community in general.

THERE IS CURRENTLY NO CURE FOR THE ZOMBIE VIRUS. DO NOT BE MISLED BY CLAIMS OF A CURE. INFECTION WILL LEAD TO THE ZOMBIC CONDITION

▶ 4 STAGES OF TRANSFORMATION

Many factors affect the rate at which a human will move through the transformation stages to develop the full-blown zombic condition. The critical factors are the quantity of infected material transferred and the size and health of the infected individual.

There have been cases where a fully grown adult with only a small infected scratch lasted over 24 hours before becoming a zombie.

In other studies, major wounds such as a zombie bite to the jugular has seen humans transforming within minutes rather than hours.

1 INFECTION
1–4 HOURS

▶ Raised temperature and flu-like symptoms.
▶ Excessive sweating.
▶ Panic attacks.
▶ An infected individual may hide any symptoms or be unaware that they have are infected.
▶ As the zombic condition develops, there will be a noticeable lack of appetite.

2 FLU SYMPTOMS
2–8 HOURS

▶ Continuation of flu-like symptoms.
▶ Reduced hearing or visual functions.
▶ A milky film over eyes (similar to cataracts in appearance).
▶ Skin will become paler.
▶ Hallucinations.
▶ Expelling gas.
▶ May still be capable of speech.
▶ Weakness and a general lack of energy.

THE SCIENCE OF ZOMBIOLOGY
METHODS OF TRANSMISSION

Dr Ahmed studied more than 300 zombie outbreaks from the post-1945 era to the present day, plotting as accurately as possible the method of transmission of the virus to each casualty. His data confirmed that over 60% of infections are caused by zombie bites.

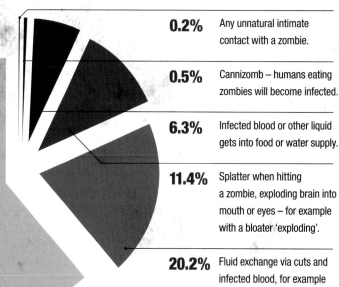

0.2% Any unnatural intimate contact with a zombie.

0.5% Cannizomb – humans eating zombies will become infected.

6.3% Infected blood or other liquid gets into food or water supply.

11.4% Splatter when hitting a zombie, exploding brain into mouth or eyes – for example with a bloater 'exploding'.

20.2% Fluid exchange via cuts and infected blood, for example a scratch from a zombie's nails.

61.4% Bite from an infected human or zombie. This is by far the most common way of transmitting the zombie virus.

3 CLINICAL DEATH
4–16 HOURS

▶ Very slow heart beat and pulse eventually ceases.
▶ Skin becomes paler, with a light blue hue in some cases.
▶ Respiration stops.
▶ All indicators point to clinical death.
▶ Body will cool quicker than a normal corpse, teeth may visibly discolour.
▶ Facebook activity will tail off.

4 ZOMBIFICATION COMPLETE
4–24 HOURS

▶ Corpse will open eyes, but breathing and heart beat will not return.
▶ Sounds include moans, groans and in some cases large discharges of trapped gas.
▶ Movement will be lumbering and slower than normal.
▶ No spoken words.
▶ The newly created zombie will attempt to consume human flesh at the first opportunity.

Dr Ahmed's Four Stages of Transformation are a generalised guideline for zombification.

THE SCIENCE OF ZOMBIOLOGY

RESEARCH IN A CRISIS

Just because you don't have any formal medical research training, doesn't mean you can't discover a cure and save the world. Science owes much to the gifted amateur.

Before toying with an apocalyptic virus try to do at least some background reading. Learn about the equipment in your lab and brush up on your basic chemistry and biology. Nothing beats learning on the job so you'll soon find out the diference between a homogeniser and a cryogenic storage dewar.

Small things like wearing a white lab coat and keeping strange hours can all help to get you 'in the mood' for research and don't be disappointed if you only manage to repeat that burning magnesium experience you remember from chemistry at school.

FACTS ABOUT THE VIRUS

▶ Virus particles are only about one-millionth of an inch (17 to 300 nanometers) long so special equipment will certainly be in order.

▶ Unlike human cells or bacteria, viruses carry only one or two enzymes that contain their genetic code. These enzymes are the 'instructions' for the transformation to the zombic condition.

▶ Viruses need a host cell. No cell, no zombie.

▶ The immune system in humans is totally overwhelmed by the zombie virus as it multiplies in the body. Extra doses of vitamin C and echinacea will not help patients.

▶ Antibiotics have no effect on a virus. They impact only on the reproduction of bacteria.

▶ MICROBIOLOGY 101

For those with the right skills and enthusiasm, searching for a cure to the 'zombie plague' could be a satisfying and potentially world-saving way to see out the zombie apocalypse. As your fellow survivors are battling dead across broken cities, you could be safely tucked away in a secret bunker, working on a cure and any other projects. You will still be playing a role in defeating the walking dead, albeit one away from any frontline action and horror. If you are not a trained virologist or research scientist then you need to get up to speed quickly on the fundamentals of curing an RNA virus. Try to learn what terms like lipid membrane and nucleic acid mean before the dead rise or you will be in for some serious cramming. The diagram below shows how the zombie virus enters and takes over a cell.

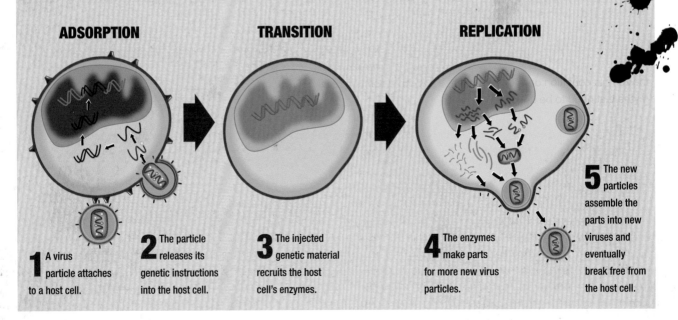

ADSORPTION **TRANSITION** **REPLICATION**

1 A virus particle attaches to a host cell.

2 The particle releases its genetic instructions into the host cell.

3 The injected genetic material recruits the host cell's enzymes.

4 The enzymes make parts for more new virus particles.

5 The new particles assemble the parts into new viruses and eventually break free from the host cell.

ZOMBIC MUTATIONS

The 'standard' dead are remorseless enough. They won't stop trying to feast on the flesh of the living, but the well-prepared zombie survivalist needs to be ready for any number of mutated and freakish creations which may surface during the zombie apocalypse.

COULD THE VIRUS MUTATE?

Viruses mutate; Fact. In 2008 over 100 people died when a mutated influenza strain of swine flu spread to humans. This ability to mutate and jump species makes some viruses virtually impossible to 'cure' in the traditional sense.

Remember, the only way the zombie virus can survive is through a host cell and, as we have accounts of zombism dating back thousands of years, it is likely that the virus has mutated many times over as the host immune system develops.

So, after all this science, could the zombie virus actually mutate? Answer: in all likelihood, it already has and continues to do so. Zombie survivalists have to be ever vigilant in identifying new symptoms or species jumps.

SUPERFAST ZOMBIES

The British horror film *28 Days Later* effectively reinvented the zombie for the twenty-first century. Gone were the shambling blue-grey walking corpses of George Romero orthodoxy. In their place we find the rebranded superfast and super violent zombie now renamed as 'the infected'. It made for a wonderful film and some decent sequels. However, in the field of zombiology, the film is much maligned for spreading misinformation across the zombie-fighting community. Sure the infected were an exciting fictional creation, but this is all they are. Zombies that have recently turned can almost match human running speeds, but over time they will slow down as the zombic condition develops. Here are a few more zombie myths that need to be quashed.

- ▶ You are unlikely to wake up in a hospital, only to find the world taken over by the dead. Chances are you will have been feasted upon long ago.
- ▶ Zombies do not run like Olympic athletes. Don't underestimate them but equally don't turn them into superhuman creatures.
- ▶ Be cautious of works of fiction when preparing for the zombie apocalypse. Some are worthy survival efforts, offering almost case-study-like accuracy. Others are pure entertainment and could lead to you preparing for a threat you will never face.

▶ MUTATION AHEAD

SIGNS TO LOOK OUT FOR

If the *X-Men* have taught us anything, it's that mutation can be both a good and a bad thing. For example, maybe the living will develop an immunity to the zombie virus or maybe the dead will lose their appetite. On the less positive side, there are five key areas you should monitor for any 'strange developments' which may indicate that the zombie virus has mutated.

ENHANCED MENTAL CAPABILITIES

Zombies have started to think or show problem-solving ability. You notice zombies gathered in a huddle, discussing plans to attack. You notice organisation in their attacks, with some creatures hanging back rather than surging forward to join the potential meat-fest.

ENHANCED PHYSICAL CAPABILITIES

Your survival vehicle is overtaken by a running zombie with a distinct cockney accent. The dead start to seriously tear into your strong wooden door with their bloody fists. Powerful shots to the chest don't even knock a zombie down, it just continues surging on towards you.

ENHANCED SENSES

You find you just can't shake off a zombie horde following you. No matter where you hide the dead develop an uncanny knack of finding you. You see the dead scanning buildings for any evidence of the living.

CLASSIC MUTATIONS

Not hard to spot, you'll see creatures unknown to God walking down the road. Any humanoid with multiple heads would be a good indicator. .

VIRUS CARRIERS

Some humans may be bitten but not develop the symptoms. Look out for survivors who have prominent bite marks on their body and yet show no sign of fever or transformation. Be aware that these individuals may still be able to transfer the virus.

THE SCIENCE OF ZOMBIOLOGY

BUILDING A SECRET LAB

Planning regulations in most countries make building a secret underground laboratory or indeed any kind of 'lair' perilously difficult. Here are the key factors you will need to consider.

▶ Location is everything. No need to buy in a central location but the geology and foundations must be right. Out-of-town and wilderness sites are ideal but may prove expensive in terms of building costs.

▶ Get expert help. Building a research bunker isn't a do-it-yourself job. There are some off-the-shelf plans available, but you will need a specialist architect and scientific advisor.

▶ Hire a building project manager that is 'on the edge'. They'll need contacts in the security industry to get the kind of kit you are going to need. They should have experience in developing top-secret projects.

▶ Try to keep neighbours and casual observers in the dark. Tell them you are building a large swimming pool or a studio for your new potter's wheel. Use screens to shield sensitive work from prying eyes.

▶ THE ULTIMATE SECRET LAB

GETTING FUNDING

To build a fully equipped secret scientific research lab, it is estimated that you will need £1–2 billion. Here are some fundraising schemes you may want to consider:

▶ **START A CHARITY** Start an anti-zombie 'save the world' charity. Get celebrities involved as they normally love this kind of thing.

▶ **CHRISTMAS SINGLE** Release a classic Christmas single. Again, remember the celebrities.

▶ **CRIME PAYS** Start a secret life of crime, amassing substantial amounts of cash.

▶ **LOOK EAST** Make contact with royal families in the Middle East, explain what you're up to and that you need a large loan.

▶ **FAMILY 'INVESTMENT'** Talk to your family. They may not understand your work, but you can always brand it as an 'investment' – technically, that's not a lie.

WORKING WITH THE DEAD

At some point during your work with the virus, you will need to collect and manage 'live' zombie specimens. Working with zombies is always a dangerous activity so ensure that you keep them sealed off where possible. Always fully destroy your test subjects and wear protective clothing when conducting experiments, including safety goggles. Never assume a zombie is dormant. Always approach them with caution.

1 Large stack of comic books.

2 Full research library with leather sofa for snoozing.

3 Well-equipped research lab.

4 Defensive automated machine gun turrets.

5 Luxury sleeping quarters.

6 Stylish communal kitchen area.

7 Automated food and drink machines.

8 Supplies for at least a decade.

9 An outside door you can open to trap zombies and other specimens.

10 Containment cells for your freakish creations.

11 A white lab coat storage area.

12 Test tube and other medical supplies area.

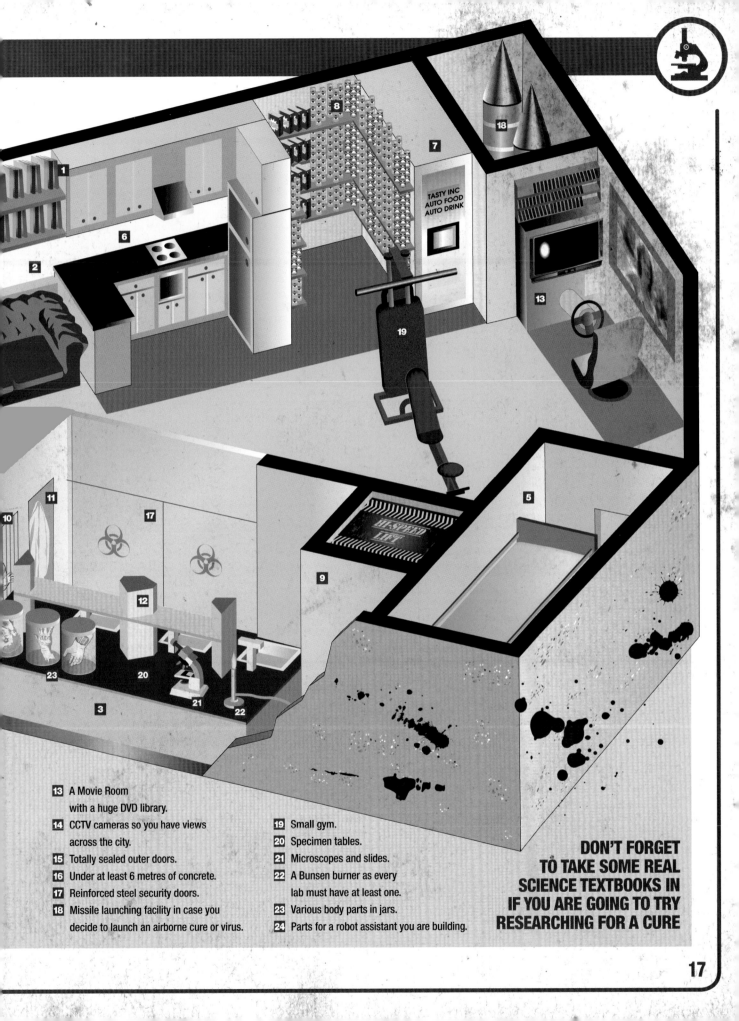

13 A Movie Room
with a huge DVD library.

14 CCTV cameras so you have views
across the city.

15 Totally sealed outer doors.

16 Under at least 6 metres of concrete.

17 Reinforced steel security doors.

18 Missile launching facility in case you
decide to launch an airborne cure or virus.

19 Small gym.

20 Specimen tables.

21 Microscopes and slides.

22 A Bunsen burner as every
lab must have at least one.

23 Various body parts in jars.

24 Parts for a robot assistant you are building.

**DON'T FORGET
TO TAKE SOME REAL
SCIENCE TEXTBOOKS IN
IF YOU ARE GOING TO TRY
RESEARCHING FOR A CURE**

THE SCIENCE OF ZOMBIOLOGY

THE ZOMBIE VIRUS AND ANIMALS

To the best of our knowledge, no animal has yet developed the zombic condition. So, for now, your pets are safe from the virus. In addition, humans with the fully developed zombic condition show little interest in non-human sources of food. In outbreaks, it has often been noted that dogs and cats can walk freely through crowds of the dead without attracting any ghoulish attention.

▶ Prepare your pet for the zombie apocalypse in the same way you would any other member of the family. Create a small Bug-Out Bag containing emergency food, chew toy and any other essentials.

▶ Keep all inoculations up to date. Do not allow your pet to become overweight and maintain a healthy diet for them.

▶ Dogs in particular can be invaluable companions during the zombie crisis. Hamsters and Guinea pigs are of less use, maybe except as decoys to distract the undead.

▶ The bovine variant of the virus has been identified as a potential source of a cure for the condition in humans so don't kill cows unless you are really desperate for a steak.

REMEMBER, WILD AND STRAY DOGS WILL BECOME A MENACE AS SOCIETY FALLS APART AND RABIES WILL ALSO BE A RISK

▶ THE MOST FEARED LIST

Developing a list of the most feared 'zombie creatures' is a regular pastime in most zombie apocalypse forums across the web. Whilst it is largely recognised that the virus does not currently transform animals or insects, zombie survivalists are a cautious crew and have prepared a list of the most deadly infected animals and insects as well as some approaches to dealing with them.

Other creatures that made the list include obvious zombie cats and dogs in common urban areas. Whereas infected chimps and orangutans will be less of a problem outside zoos and parts of the world where they still exist in the wild.

If you are engaged in any research, do not test on animals. Not only is it cruel, there is also a chance that you may stumble upon a mutated virus and cause all kinds of problems for other survivors. If you do need 'live' test subjects then you will need to develop a canny ruse to lure them into your lair. The Ministry of Zombies does not sanction any testing on humans, but if you are desperate, you can always use your lab assistant – it's what they're for.

CURRENTLY, THERE ARE NO CONFIRMED CASES OF ANIMALS, BIRDS OR INSECTS CONTRACTING THE ZOMBIC CONDITION OR TRANSFERRING THE INFECTION

MOST FEARED
THE Z-SHARK

The Z-Shark is the top of most lists. Take one of the world's most highly developed hunters, make it pretty much invincible and give all breeds an even greater taste for human flesh. Few would go near the water with such killers on the prowl. However, in reality the zombie virus could dull a shark's keen sense of smell and taste. It could have serious issues with direction and some experts picture the mentally-reduced creatures just floating to the surface, unable to function. Let's hope we never have to find out.

THE SCIENCE OF ZOMBIOLOGY
THE RISK OF ANIMAL MUTATION

The zombie virus is an incredibly complex and adaptable RNA virus and there is every possibility that it could one day mutate and affect animals. In tests, it has been shown that pets from outbreak areas are actually carrying the virus in their blood but for some reason do not develop the zombic condition which blights humans. For example, studies of an outbreak in Aleppo in Syria during the 1990s revealed that over 90% of cats and dogs in the city carried the virus in their blood and yet there were no reports of any infected pets or animals. In a post-apocalyptic world, it is best to keep clear of any stray animals and avoid the risk of infections such as rabies.

RUSSIANS AND AN INFECTED CHIMP

In 2008, documents were posted across the web reporting that Russian scientists working on a cure for the zombie virus had successfully infected a primate with the zombic condition. If true, this would be the first documented case of an animal developing and turning zombic. Some grainy photos of the primate have been leaked and can be seen on the internet, but in blurry black and white it's hard to make anything out other than the outline of an ape and a banana.

> THE MEDIA FRENZY AROUND THE ANTI-VIRAL NATALIA_739 IS AT BEST SPECULATION AND AT WORST MISLEADING JOURNALISM. THERE IS CURRENTLY NO EVIDENCE THAT ANIMALS CAN BE INFECTED WITH THE ZOMBIE VIRUS.

KIND OF FEARED
ZOMBIE RATS OR ZATS

Imagine their tiny feet scurrying around, overrunning every town and city. See hundreds of infected red eyes watching you from the shadows and emerging to munch on your toes as you sleep. With their numbers and size, infected rodents could become a serious threat to survivor communities. They are unlikely to be distracted by a cube of cheese (unless it's blood-soaked) and will be fiendish to kill. The one consolation again is that the zombie condition will slow them down and reduce their well-known cunning to the level of Baldrick from the *Black Adder* TV series.

STILL FEARED
ZOMBIE MOSQUITOES

Forget anything large; if these zombic flyers stick their diseased proboscis into your flesh and transmit the virus directly into your blood stream, it's curtains for everyone. Many areas of the world are infested with these insects, or similar biting fiends, and you will need more than bug spray to eliminate them. In addition, the collapse of civilisation and drainage, flooding may create new habitats for this potentially deadly foe. However, in all probability it is thought that a viral jump into insects is the least likely scientific outcome – probably.

ZOMBIES IN HISTORY

The most common question asked by those sceptical about the walking dead is why there are not accounts of zombie outbreaks in history? After all, if the zombie virus has been with us for thousands of years, why aren't our history books peppered with accounts of the dead?

The real answer is remarkably simple. The rotting claw of the zombie touches human history at virtually every key point, but up to now it has rarely been acknowledged and on even fewer occasions studied. A comprehensive survey of zombic incidents has yet to be completed, but when it is, it will document outbreaks of the zombic condition from before the Ice Age.

The oldest known reference to the walking dead is in the surviving fragments of the Sumer myth-tale *The Epic of Gilgamesh* which outlines that the dead intend to 'go up to eat the living'. This is a clear reference to the cannibalistic symptoms of someone infected with the zombie virus.

Recently discovered cave paintings in the south of France show heavy-set and lumbering figures attacking fleeing cave dwellers and, in some sections, tearing and feasting on the limbs of the living. Some human-like figures can clearly be seen battling the dead, but the overall feel is one of terror, with the living scattering to escape the hungry corpses. As for the zombies themselves, they are almost stylised caricatures of the dead, painted with arms out front and typically oversized in comparison to their human prey.

ZOMBIE TIMELINE

In 2009, a pioneering group of zombie experts and academics met at Oxford University for a three-day conference on zombies in history. The outcome of one of the study groups was the world's first timeline of zombie incidents across the history of civilisation. Those familiar with zombie history will immediately note the absence of several key episodes such as the walking dead outbreak in Essex in 1934 and the New York City plague of 1948. To be included in this official timeline, the outbreak needed to be confirmed by at least two documented sources and pass through the rigours of a historical investigation.

1064
An outbreak in the Normandy countryside sets back William, the Duke of Normandy's invasion plans almost three years as he attempts to control what he later referred to as a 'Saxon ruse'. Contemporary accounts see William employing expensive mercenaries from across Europe to deal with the incident. See the diaries of Brother Thomas of Rouen for further details.

3000 BC
Eypytian hieroglyphics on Rameses II tombs shows lumbering figures being beheaded. Images of the 'undead' are common themes across the Middle Kingdom and several vases in the British Museum carry clear images of the walking dead.

55
Philosper Aristocles muses that there is 'something of hades' about some dead villagers. His was the first documented account of a zombie outbreak in Western history and was corroborated by Greek poet Herodicus in his *Journals of Adventure*.

797
Chinese general Wei-Lang uses infected blood to poison a rival warlord. He later employed the walking dead as an army to ravage his southern rivals and create one of the largest and most powerful kingdoms in China.

1576
Venetians isolate a 'zombie colony' on the cemetery island of San Michele. The site was closed to the public right up until it was razed to the ground by fire in 1933.

ZOMBIES IN HISTORY
ZOMBIE ACHIEVEMENTS

Many experienced zombie fighters will clock up literally hundreds of 'kills' as they battle their way through legions of the walking dead. Dispatching zombies will become second nature as the number dealt with rises.

However, we have already learnt that zombies are both persistent and resilient. It is easy for fighters to start underestimating their opponents. Zombies have achieved incredible things in history – maybe they haven't won any medals but they are lethal killers, either in groups or solo.

ZOMBIE SPEED

In 2002, US forces in Afghanistan were attacked by what soldiers later referred to as 'running corpses'. According to official reports, the crazed individuals ran alongside moving vehicles and were clocked at over 20 miles per hour.

The Ministry of Zombies debriefed several of the soldiers involved in this report and, although unconfirmed, it is believed that the climatic conditions and recent outbreak of the zombie virus in a nearby village enabled a corpse to run at an extremely fast rate. Typically the dead cannot reach these speeds, but on this occasion they would have given an Olympic sprinter a run for his money.

ZOMBIE ENDURANCE

In 2001, a number of national newspapers in South Korea reported that a 'cannibal lunatic' had crept into an apartment block in the city of Anyang. Once inside the secure building, he murdered 10 residents before being taken out by an 87-year-old grandmother, Mrs Park, who later told a local news channel of her suspicions.

Investigations by the Ministry of Zombies in South Korea have shown that the zombie in question crawled through nearly a mile of drainage pipes to gain access to the block.

The energetic Mrs Park went on to establish the Just Block It foundation in 2005, which aims to raise awareness of zombie-related drainage pipe attacks. In 2010, her tireless work finally bore fruit as legislation was introduced into the South Korean lower house to limit the diameter of any new drainage pipes fitted. As a result, from 2015 onwards, all new builds in the republic will have zombie-proof water and drainage systems.

> **THAT WAS NO MAN. IT CAME UP THROUGH THE SEWER PIPES. IT DIDN'T HAVE ANY LEGS AND I KILLED IT THE ONLY WAY YOU CAN WITH THESE CREATURES. I BLUDGEONED IT OVER THE HEAD WITH MY WALKING STICK**

MRS PARK, SOUTH KOREA

1665

An outbreak of zombies in Devon, England masks the arrival of the bubonic plague and before the disease is recognised, infected corpses have reached as far as Coventry. Before its destruction in the Second World War, Coventry Cathedral contained a mass tomb known as the 'grave of lost souls'. It is said that zombies were hurled into this grave just before the plague struck the city.

1921

Famous psychologist Sigmund Freud completed his controversial work *The Importance of Ghoulies*, in which he questioned a sexual motive behind the desire of the zombie to feed on living humans. Freud was forced to release it himself as a pamphlet. Few copies now remain, but one is available for public viewing at the Library of Congress in Vienna, Austria.

2001

Dr Khalid Ahmed isolates the zombie virus for the first time and goes on to develop the first model of zombic infection. He pioneered the mapping of symptoms over time and is widely regarded as the father of zombiology.

1780

After offending a fellow noble at a court event, the well-known French dandy the Comte de Menthe was challenged to a duel. As was the convention at the time, he duly appointed a second to fight the duel and several observers noted that this man was not stopped by either a pistol ball or a rapier strike and went on to 'feast on the defeated gentlemen'.

1999

Virologist Dr Raymond Carter creates his model of zombie infection by using computers to model a global outbreak, but it is not until 2009 that Carter finally develops the comprehensive theory of meta-hordes, in which he predicts vast, swirling swarms of the dead, numbering in their tens of millions, sweeping entire countries clean of any living survivors. This theory was novelised in 2011 in the work *Meta-Horde*.

ZOMBIES IN HISTORY

HISTORICAL ACCOUNTS

As a result of the 2009 Oxford University symposium on the walking dead, historians have begun to research specific incidents in zombie history in far more depth. New discoveries in the field of zombie science have enabled them to take a fresh look at the contemporary records and uncover the truth behind some of these mysterious outbreaks. The first volume in an official zombie history is due to be published in 2015 and will be *A Zombie History of Europe*, with further volumes to follow. But for now, zombie fighters should study these accounts to learn lessons from how our ancestors battled the dead. Three of the best examples have been examined and offer insight into surviving a zombie siege, battling bloaters and advanced combat tactics.

27 BC–476 AD
ROMAN EMPIRE

The Roman Empire encountered many threats in its long history across the ages, but none was more persistent or dangerous than outbreaks of the zombie virus.

The Romans were the first to document the symptoms of the zombic condition and suffered periodic outbreaks from 55 AD through to the last years of the empire.

In 100 AD, philosopher, mathematician and scientist Agrippa Aquila recorded the following:

'IT IS WITHOUT QUESTION THE WICKED VAPOURS OF THE RIONE MONTI WHICH CAUSE THIS AFFLICTION. IT SEEMS TO PRAY ON THE DESTITUTE AND DEPRAVED. AND, IF OUR EXPERIENCE HAS TAUGHT US ANYTHING, IT IS TO STAMP OUT THESE DISEASED VERMIN WHEREVER THEY CRAWL WITHIN OUR LANDS.'

Their grasp of the science was tenuous at best, but the Romans were brutal in their treatment of any citizen or slave found to be suffering with the zombic 'affliction'. Death was the only option. Contemporary accounts talk of legionnaires brutally clearing whole quarters of the city to quell an outbreak. For the Romans, it wasn't a question of being brutal. They realised that if the zombic condition took hold of a populous area, they would be powerless to defeat it.

1923
AUSTRALIA

Rural backwater Bramwell Station in Cape York Peninsula, Australia become front-page news in 1923 after a major zombie outbreak led to the army being deployed to bring the dead under control.

One of the most famous survival accounts from this episode became known as the Siege at Macgregor's Farm and was serialised in both the *London* and *New York Times*. The events latter become the subject of the 1947 book *Through War, Zombies and Depression*.

With their isolated farmstead under siege for almost a week by over 80 zombies, the courageous Macgregors dug in and defended their home with whatever weapons they had to hand. They hammered planks over every door and window and carefully managed their supplies in near-unbearable tropical heat and humidity before being finally liberated.

The plucky Miranda Macgregor went on to publish the details of the siege in her memoir some years later.

'WE SHOWED EVERYTHING WE AUSSIES ARE PROUD OF IN THAT BLOODY SIEGE. WE FOUGHT ALONG, KEPT OUR SPIRITS UP AND RELIED ON OUR OWN SUPPLIES. NEVER ONCE DID WE THINK ABOUT GIVING UP, NOT EVEN WHEN THE DEAD WERE BANGING ON EVERY WINDOW AND DOOR.'

1964
VIETNAM

It was the US Army in Vietnam that first documented what are known in zombie-fighting circles as 'bloaters'. The tropical conditions led to infected corpses swelling up to four times their original size. The resulting creatures are slow and cumbersome but are prone to spew out infected bile and innards if they are shot or punctured, making them particularly dangerous in close combat.

US ARMY'S THREE RULES FOR BATTLING BLOATERS (MILITARY DOCUMENT 1964)

1. Maintain at least 10 yards from the infected party.
2. Do not direct fire to the bloated mid-section – go for a target head or limb shot.
3. Shoot within 5 yards and you will be infected by the resulting explosion of material.

► ROMANS vs THE DEAD (BELLATOR MORTIS)

The Roman Empire learnt from a series of zombie outbreaks as their territory expanded and made major changes from how they structured their army units to developing the world's first zombie public awareness campaign.

After some early defeats, the Roman military machine quickly learnt that it needed to adapt to fight such a porous and disorganised but fearless enemy. Borrowing military wisdom from their Greek neighbours, Roman legions engaged in anti-zombie operations were restructured from a fixed, heavy infantry approach into smaller and more manoeuvrable units. The reforms saw the basic unit of infantry reduced and new defensive strategies emerge.

I ORGANISATION

Small, more moveable, units of five rather than the standard eight, making them far more flexible and able to respond more quickly to the movements of their dead opponents.

II DEFENCE

Heavy emphasis on defensive shield training, with units forming a complete wall to keep out the zombies. They also spent hours practising with a long stabbing sword, which was designed to keep the dead at arms' length.

III MOVEMENT

Roman soldiers were very fit. Trained to do slow trots over 22 miles called 'dead marches' to escape the dead.

IV WEAPONS

Introduction of the 'Gladius Mortus' sword of the dead – which was long and heavier than the traditional gladius.

Deadly sling shot.

'A STONE TO THE HEAD, DEALS WITH THE DEAD.'

V POSTERS

Public warning posters all around Pompeii.

THE ZOMBIE APOCALYPSE

A main theme of this book is about preparing for a zombie outbreak. Most outbreaks are localised, with maybe a few hundred zombies running riot until they are dealt with. You need to have the information and training to survive such an incident.

However, most zombie experts now agree that it is a case of when and not if the world sees a major zombie outbreak – a time when a zombie outbreak expands at an exponential rate and the number of dead soon dwarfs that of the living. This will mean the collapse of civilisation, effectively the end of the humans as top of the food chain. This is a zombie apocalypse.

IF THE VIRUS HAS BEEN AROUND FOR YEARS, WHY SHOULD WE BE WORRIED ABOUT THE ZOMBIE APOCALYPSE NOW?

The world's population has grown to almost 8 billion and as the number of people increases so does the chance of a zombie outbreak. The urbanised areas have rapidly increased in the last 50 years, spawning sprawling super-cities such as Cairo, Beijing and New York. The densely packed crowds are ideal greenhouses for a major outbreak. In addition, globalisation and the growth of international air travel now means that an infected individual could be half way across the world before they get the munchies.

10 REASONS TO BE WORRIED

Top entertainment and fashion magazine asked over 10,000 readers this question – why should people be concerned about zombies taking over the world?

1. Getting eaten alive would be awful.
2. Seeing a relative or close friend getting eaten wouldn't be fun.
3. Being attacked by desperate survivors or looters.
4. None of my favourite TV shows would be on.
5. I might be turned into one of the dead and I'm vegetarian so I'd get hungry.
6. My social life would dry up more than normal.
7. No Facebook – the photos may not be as nice.
8. Shops would be closed and I can't bear wearing last year's fashions.
9. I might be stuck with a group of ugly survivors.
10. There'd be no one left to read the saucy new novel I'm writing about a girl in the city and her adventures in bondage.

MANY OF THE GENERAL PUBLIC HAVE NO UNDERSTANDING OF WHAT A ZOMBIE APOCALYPSE WOULD REALLY MEAN

ZOMBIES IN HISTORY THINGS I WOULD DO?

In 2009 a research team conducted over 800 in-depth interviews with members of the public asking them what they'd do in the event of a zombie apocalypse.

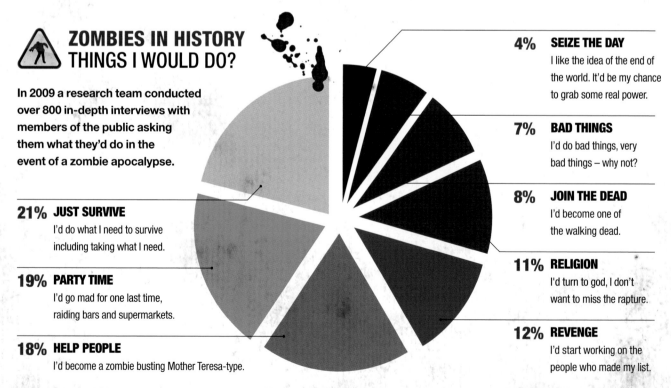

21% JUST SURVIVE
I'd do what I need to survive including taking what I need.

19% PARTY TIME
I'd go mad for one last time, raiding bars and supermarkets.

18% HELP PEOPLE
I'd become a zombie busting Mother Teresa-type.

4% SEIZE THE DAY
I like the idea of the end of the world. It'd be my chance to grab some real power.

7% BAD THINGS
I'd do bad things, very bad things – why not?

8% JOIN THE DEAD
I'd become one of the walking dead.

11% RELIGION
I'd turn to god, I don't want to miss the rapture.

12% REVENGE
I'd start working on the people who made my list.

► ZOMBIE APOCALYPSE WARNING SCALE

INTERNATIONALLY RECOGNISED SCALE

Of course not every zombie outbreak will, as they call it, 'go septic' but from our survey work, it is clear that widespread panic means you must prepare now and use a warning sign to give advance notice that the dead are on the rise. Luckily, the field of zombiology has an internationally recognised scale of outbreaks.

CREATING YOUR OWN WARNING SCALE

► A few hours a week will keep you on top of developments.
► Build up local contacts with police, fire and ambulance services for inside information.
► Use informal networks of zombie spotters on the web.
► Have something on the wall like a whiteboard and use a traffic light system to indicate your level of alertness.

RATING	CONDITIONS AND WHAT TO EXPECT	WHAT YOU SHOULD DO?	PERSONALISED PLAN (EXAMPLE)
Zed-Con 5 - All Clear	► Condition normal. ► The zombie virus has always been in the population but is currently latent with no reported sufferers of the zombic condition.	► Remain vigilant. ► Keep emergency supplies stocked up. ► Continue to monitor multiple new channels.	- Mrs Lowe acting strangely – zombie or just drunk? - CNN article about cannibalism in France. - Will record for review later.
Zed-Con 4 Localised Outbreak	► Localised outbreak or so-called 'ghoul infestation'. ► 90% of such outbreaks are dealt with below the radar of official government. ► Most Zed-Con 4 incidents will involve fewer than one hundred zombies.	► Check in with local doctor – any extra reports of unexplained flu-like viruses? ► Check police radio for crimes involving cannibalism.	- Small outbreak in China on web – am monitoring. - Took day off work to monitor developments. - Cancelled Disney trip. Kids not happy.
Zed-Con 3 Regional Outbreak	► A more significant outbreak, often involving more than one village or a small town. ► Zombie numbers are typically 1000+. ► Expect army intervention, road blocks and stories of 'industrial accidents'.	► No matter where it is in the world, prepare for lockdown. ► Keep your fellow survivors updated.	- Checked off all stocks. - Called all of survivor group. - Preparing for lockdown.
Zed-Con 2 National Outbreak	► Several cities or provinces are dominated by zombies. ► The country will be under martial law. ► Information will be unreliable. ► Zombie numbers are typically 10,000+.	► Last chance to check on any elderly neighbours. ► Risk foraging only if you are missing something vital.	- Full lockdown. - Emergency broadcasts report all roads closed. - Implementing 90-day plan.
Zed-Con 1 Global Pandemic	► World travel and communication breaks down. ► Governments and central authority will crumble. ► More and more countries will turn 'grey' as the zombies take over.	► Deliver strong leadership. ► Go through the 90-day survival plan again. ► Deal with any of the dead who take an interest in your home.	- This is the big one! - Re-checked all stocks. - Took out two zombies trying to get into the garden. Good to get my first kills. Me 2 Zombies 0!

BECOMING A ZOMBIE SURVIVALIST

Let's be honest here – if you are doing nothing to prepare for the zombie apocalypse, your chances of surviving more than three months in a nation overrun by the dead are extremely small – in fact, it's less than 0.005%. That's a fact.

If these facts tell us anything, it's that you'd better change your mindset and start preparing for the zombies now. Either that or become a drunken millionaire pilot who has been given haemorrhoids by Satan after slipping in the shower and whose plane fell to pieces just before he was canonised.

Before lurching into depression, it's worth noting that moderate changes to your lifestyle and circumstances can drastically improve your chances of survival. For example, simple factors such as keeping a Bug-Out Bag of supplies handy, keeping fit and reading up on the walking dead, can all start to decrease the likelihood of you becoming a cheap meat snack in the first few days. Your aim is to be one of the zombie survivalists to make it through. And, right here is where you have to start. You need to address four key areas to be the complete zombie survivalist.

WHAT ARE MY CHANCES OF:

1 in 25	Getting haemorrhoids
1 in 117	Being on plane with a drunken pilot
1 in 215	Dating a millionaire
1 in 2,232	Fatally slipping in a bath or shower
1 in 7,000	Being considered possessed by Satan
1 in 20,000	Surviving the zombie apocalypse without preparation
1 in 10,000,000	Dying from parts falling off an airplane
1 in 20,000,000	Odds of getting canonised
1 in 43,000,000	Being hit by a burning meteor
1 in 52,000,000	Being killed by a falling fridge

AREAS TO ADDRESS

AREA 1
MENTALITY

You must want to survive. If you can't survive without the latest slice of reality TV, you may as well give up. With the world going to hell around you, you need to be 100% convinced that you want to survive and prosper. This is known as the 'survival mentality' and you can't order it online.

AREA 2
KNOWLEDGE

You must understand the threats you face and seize any opportunities. Know your enemy, their tactics and weaknesses. Review the likely impact on your country and local area and plan accordingly. Read reliable outbreak accounts and become familiar with how things pan out when the dead come to town.

HOW TO BE 'ZOMBIE' STREET SMART

In later chapters, you will learn how to defend yourself against the dead, but there is much you can do before the dead rise to ensure that you are mentally prepared for the challenges ahead. Any formal military, outbound or firearms training are obvious choices as are camping, cooking and gardening as key subjects that will help you survive. It's also important that you start to develop a survivor mentality – that you become Zombie Street Smart. No survival book will teach you how to be Zombie Street Smart. Sure, you can learn about the threats and look for the right signs, but true zombie awareness is about maintaining that level of vigilance at all times. Here are some pointers:

▶ **Know your neighbourhood.** Always think about where zombies could be lurking and how to get home safely.

▶ **Always keep your eyes open** – never walk along listening to music or you may miss the moan of an approaching zombie.

▶ **Always have an escape route** – no matter where you are, at work, on the train, at the store – remember how you came in and have an alternative escape route.

▶ **Be on the lookout for signs of the zombic condition** – grey skin, milky eyes, feverish and with an unhealthy interest in eating the flesh of others.

▶ **Tell as many people as you can about the threat of the zombies.** Who knows, you might save someone's life?

As you become more zombie street smart, you will start to develop what zombie preppers refer to as a 'hyper awareness' of anything zombic. You'll find you're always watching for those tell-tale signs and start to see the walking dead around every corner.

10 SIGNS YOU ARE READY TO BE A ZOMBIE SURVIVALIST

As your training progresses and you learn new survival skills, you will acquire 'rep' or a reputation amongst the zombie survival community. You'll find that other experts will willingly share their experience with a fellow enthusiast. However, as others find out about your curious training regime, some at work or school may begin to treat you as a bit of a 'nut' or 'weirdo'. Do not let this put you off – you'll have the last laugh when these individuals are being mauled by zombies and you are safely barricaded in at home.

1 You have become known at work as the 'zombie guy or gal'.

2 You're actually quite looking forward to it all kicking off so you can try out your kit.

3 Work colleagues see flu, you see possible zombie virus when someone turns up at work with a slight fever.

4 When booking holidays, you think carefully about the impact if you are caught abroad.

5 You spend more than two hours a week on your homemade zombie monitoring graph.

6 Your kids have mini Bug-Out Bags to take to school.

7 You think of *Dawn of the Dead* as a training video.

8 You scan the TV channels for anything zombie related.

9 You had a serious discussion with a friend in which you tried to convince them about the threat.

10 When in the DIY centre, you see possibilities everywhere for ramping up your home defences.

AREA 3
TRAINING

Knowledge must be supported by practical experience. Obviously, it may be hard for you to find zombies to practise your fighting skills on, but there are plenty of outdoor survival, first aid and gardening courses available for you to acquire invaluable experience before the dead turn up.

AREA 4
AWARENESS

You must have a monitoring system up and running at all times. Monitor the news channels, the internet and stay in touch with fellow zombie survivalists to keep an eye on events around the world. People you may once have considered 'nuts' may become some of your best friends as you make your way through the 'zombie preppers' world.

BECOMING A ZOMBIE SURVIVALIST

GETTING THE LOOK

Never forget that you will not be able to flick a switch and suddenly become a zombie survivalist when the zombies arrive – we are talking about a mentality here – you must live and breathe zombie survival. This may involve some real changes in your lifestyle and certainly your wardrobe. The Ministry of Zombies advises a three-step approach to get this right:

▶ **BECOMING A HARD GUY OR GAL**
▶ **THE ZOMBIE SURVIVALIST LOOK**
  – PRE-APOCALYPSE
▶ **THE ZOMBIE SURVIVALIST LOOK**
  – ONCE THE OUTBREAK BEGINS!

▶ BECOMING A HARD GUY OR GAL

Surviving the zombies is not just about fighting the dead, it's about being able to look after yourself, so developing a new 'kick ass' personality now is a great way to start. Here are six ways you can get that 'hard' look:

1 Do scary things like abseiling and show no fear about anything. Never admit to being afraid of heights or spiders. You need to become known as a fearless type, with a little of the loose cannon about you.

2 Use a 'hard man' walk whether you are male or female – that confident swagger will ensure that all will take notice.

3 Use silence skilfully. Don't talk too much and never ask for help. When you do talk, use short and slightly mysterious sentences, hinting that you have seen a lot but don't want to talk about it.

4 Use every opportunity to reinforce the general perception that you are tough – for example, never complain of a headache or toothache. Throw in the occasional phrase like – 'I think I broke a rib this morning at my full contact kickboxing class.' Then wait for the shock response and reply coolly, 'It's not the first time.'

5 Don't start fights but if you are in action, make sure you are the one who finishes it.

6 Use every opportunity to show what a hard nut you are by helping others and playing the knight in shining armour, but look cool whilst doing it. Rarely smile.

These top tips can help you build a 'tough' persona and, when combined with your strict training regime, it will not be long before you develop what is known as a 'Rambo personality'.

▶ THE ZOMBIE SURVIVALIST LOOK

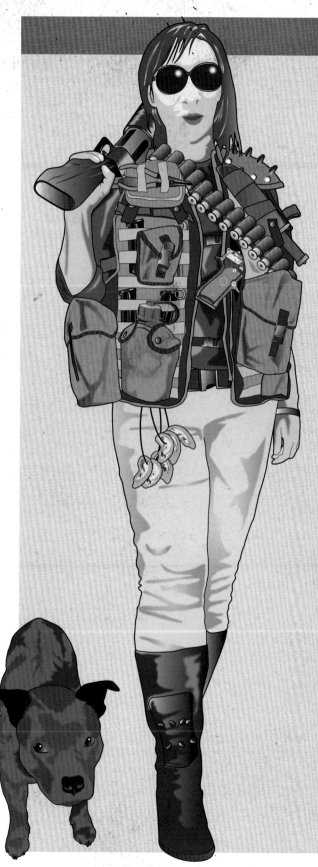

PRE-APOCALYPSE

In most countries, it's just not possible to live every day looking like an extra from a *Mad Max* movie. However, you should support your new persona with a kick-ass look. Here are five pointers on how to dress:

1. Boots always work so wear them; black combat boots can give you that tough edge.
2. Tear the sleeves off your shirt and wear jeans with rips and holes in them. Never button a shirt all the way up.
3. Try a worn-out black leather jacket and combat or cargo pants combo – never wear a skirt (unless you're a Scotsman) – particularly if you are male.
4. Sport a mean and intimidating look on your face to go with the outfit. Practise this in the mirror to avoid looking as if you are unwell or constipated.
5. Finally, get the hair right – generally styles which require a hairdryer will not help. If you are female, you must avoid looking like Tina Turner in *Mad Max Beyond Thunderdome*.

ONCE THE OUTBREAK BEGINS!

Once the outbreak starts, it's time to put all of your training and preparation into action. You can now change into your full zombie apocalypse outfit, including weapons and accessories. Armed with these and your new hard persona you will drastically increase your chances of surviving.

▶ Stylish headband.
▶ Steel toe caps.
▶ Decent walking boots.
▶ 'Kick ass' haircut.
▶ Cool shades.
▶ A perfected mean stance.
▶ Adorned in weapons.
▶ A light pack for supplies and any loot.
▶ Leather jacket with studs.
▶ Optional severed zombies ears for extra 'hardness' appeal.
▶ Must have the right name – not Kevin or Dave.
▶ Walking the delicate line between hard case and camp.
▶ Carrying a gun even if it's empty.
▶ Good belt with useful accessory compartments.
▶ A mean stare which says 'don't mess with me'.
▶ Post-apoc dog companion optional.

THINK TOUGH, LOOK TOUGH AND STAY TOUGH!

BECOMING A ZOMBIE SURVIVALIST

BE READY OR BE DEAD!

The Bug-Out Bag is a feature of every good survival guide but the Ministry of Zombies has pioneered the creation of an entire system to help you and your family survive a zombie apocalypse.

The Bug-Out System is an emergency set of procedures to ensure that you make the best possible start when the dead rise. It consists of three main elements.

▶ **BUG-OUT BAG**
▶ **BUG-OUT LOCATION**
▶ **BUG-OUT PLAN**

In essence, the Bug-Out Bag should contain emergency supplies to get you through the first 24–48 hours of any zombie crisis. Your Bug-Out Locations are either safe houses or bolt holes you can reach in case you get caught away from your main secure location. Your Bug-Out Plan draws the two parts above together in a maintenance schedule for the Plan together with any maps, guides or routes you have planned. If you are already at home, it should be in an easy-to-reach location. If your home base is overrun, it's what you grab when you 'bug out'.

▶ CREATING A BUG-OUT BAG

The purpose of a Bug-Out Bag is to provide you with the tools and resources to make it through the first 48 hours. It is a common mistake that newly trained zombie survivalists often make to overload their bags, packing them full of everything from extra ammunition to some light reading to help make any periods in hiding bearable. Let's be clear: over packing your Bug-Out Bag will get you killed. If it significantly slows you down or hampers your movement, the statistics show that you are far more likely to be eaten by the dead.

'STAY LIGHT, STAY MOBILE AND STAY ALIVE'

Here are the suggested contents for a typical 'at work' Bug-Out Bag. This is something office workers can easily carry on their daily commutes.

⚠ **LEGAL ADVICE**

THE CONTENTS OF YOUR BUG-OUT BAG MUST MEET ANY LEGAL REQUIREMENTS IN YOUR COUNTRY. CARRYING AN INAPPROPRIATE COCKTAIL OF PETROL BOMBS AND OTHER WEAPONS IS NOT ADVISED WHERE LOCAL LAWS DO NOT ALLOW.

BECOMING A ZOMBIE SURVIVALIST
ADVICE FOR THOSE WITH DISABILITIES

Preparation is vital for anyone looking to survive in a land of the dead, but there are some additional challenges for those with disabilities. For example, your Bug-Out Plan, and indeed all survival planning, will need to take into account any special medical or physical requirements.

In terms of Bug-Out preparation, it is recommended that any bag must be light enough to carry easily. So if you have to take out some contents, simply trim down the list or look for lighter alternatives. Equally, aids such as a wheelchair or walking stick may present useful opportunities to conceal a weapon in clear view.

The Ministry of Zombies advises against using any internationally recognised signals for help, such as a white blanket hung from the window. There will be many desperate people out there ready to take advantage of a carefully prepared survivor.

With the right preparation, those with disabilities have very much the same chance as others to make it through the zombie apocalypse. The important thing is to complete a thorough needs assessment and then ensure that any resulting recommendations are integrated with your survival plan.

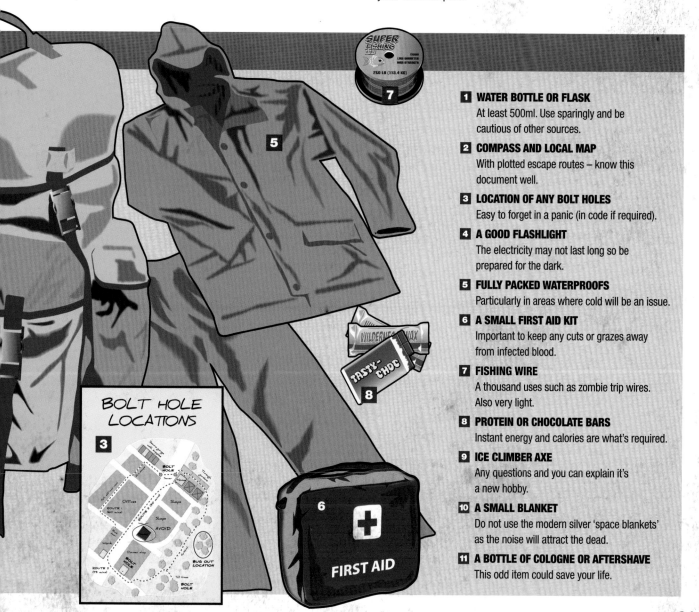

1 WATER BOTTLE OR FLASK
At least 500ml. Use sparingly and be cautious of other sources.

2 COMPASS AND LOCAL MAP
With plotted escape routes – know this document well.

3 LOCATION OF ANY BOLT HOLES
Easy to forget in a panic (in code if required).

4 A GOOD FLASHLIGHT
The electricity may not last long so be prepared for the dark.

5 FULLY PACKED WATERPROOFS
Particularly in areas where cold will be an issue.

6 A SMALL FIRST AID KIT
Important to keep any cuts or grazes away from infected blood.

7 FISHING WIRE
A thousand uses such as zombie trip wires. Also very light.

8 PROTEIN OR CHOCOLATE BARS
Instant energy and calories are what's required.

9 ICE CLIMBER AXE
Any questions and you can explain it's a new hobby.

10 A SMALL BLANKET
Do not use the modern silver 'space blankets' as the noise will attract the dead.

11 A BOTTLE OF COLOGNE OR AFTERSHAVE
This odd item could save your life.

BECOMING A ZOMBIE SURVIVALIST

▶ BUG-OUT LOCATIONS

Bug-Out Location typically refers to a secondary site you and your survivor group can relocate to if your primary location is overrun. But it also refers to any pre-checked 'safe' site you have scoped out.

LOCATIONS TO AVOID

During a major zombie outbreak, chaos and destruction will fill towns and cities. Hundreds of thousands of civilians will be unprepared when the walking dead stagger into view. It is estimated by the Ministry of Zombies that law and order as we know it will break down in most urban areas within 72 hours. With this in mind, some locations should certainly be ruled out as safe places to hide from the zombies.

PLACE OF WORSHIP

A shelter in times of trouble for many, a veritable buffet feast for the zombies. Expect carnage as church or temple goers rush to these sites.

HOSPITALS AND CLINICS

The front line of war against a virus. Unfortunately, with the zombie virus it's a war we've already lost. Avoid like the plague and expect these sites to be overrun with fresh zombies as people are brought in with the zombic condition already developing.

AIRPORTS AND DOCKS

Take rush hour and multipl it a hundred times, then add in thousands of infected. Trying to catch a plane or boat to safety will be almost impossible after the first hours of the crisis. Most zombie survivalists assume that long-distance travel of any kind will be impossible.

CAUGHT ABROAD?

Most travel insurance companies will regard zombie attacks as 'acts of nature' and such events are therefore largely excluded from most policies. If, however, you are on holiday, or away on business, during a zombie incident, the current guideline is to barricade yourself in either your hotel room or a nearby friendly embassy.

Do not attempt to reach an airport or railway station. Expect roads to be gridlocked. It is advisable that you learn 'I'm not one of them' in the relevant language.

The People's Republic of China is currently the only country with an official anti-zombie policy. For any reported sightings or if you are trapped by the dead in this country, please call:

(+86) (0) (10) 5100 4066

This is the call centre supporting the 422nd Infantry Division, which manages all zombic events in China.

COMMUNICATION CARDS

The Ministry of Zombies has developed a set of cards, which can be used to communicate in a zombie crisis in any country. They are available in various sizes and can be used if you are stranded in a country and have little grasp of the local language. If you are caught in this situation, do not panic; just slowly hold your card up. Zombie fighting groups around the world have been trained to recognise these symbols.

▶ **ZOMBIES ARE COMING!**
▶ **I'M NOT A ZOMBIE!**
▶ **LET'S JOIN TOGETHER AND FIGHT ZOMBIES**

ZOMBIE SUPPORT CARD

ZOMBIES ARE COMING!

ZOMBIE SUPPORT CARD

I'M NOT A ZOMBIE!

ZOMBIE SUPPORT CARD

JOIN TOGETHER AND FIGHT

▶ BUG-OUT PLAN

Your Bug-Out Plan should include a list of well-scouted locations to cover your immediate area and routes. Walk your target routes slowly, checking for any potential hazards and making notes of any safe bolt holes you may be able to use. Remember that during the zombie apocalypse your route is likely to be heaving with panicky crowds and even looters.

▶ Prepare your own Bug-Out Bag. You may have a version to keep at work or in the car.
▶ Assess the needs of the family and friends you plan to survive with (if any).
▶ Secure your home location. See the 90-Day Survival Plan from the Ministry of Zombies.
▶ Identify at least three routes back to your home location from your place of work and any other sites you frequent. Print and laminate routes if necessary and know them by heart.
▶ Target several 'bolt holes' along your routes to ensure that you have a temporary location should the situation on the ground prove 'too hot'. Typical examples would include hidden drainage ditches, empty homes or copses of trees.
▶ Take the time to build a list of at least two 'alpha sites'. These are locations which you have scouted and should be known to all members of your group. If you are overrun, this is where you meet up. They can be anything from a secure lock-up garage complete with spare supplies and weapons, to a well-known wood in which your scattered party can regroup in the trees.

DON'T BECOME A CHEAP MEAT SNACK FOR THE ZOMBIES. PREPARE NOW!

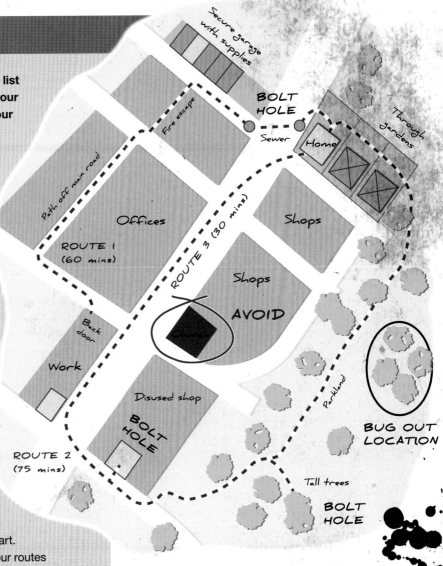

ZOMBIE PREPAREDNESS JOURNAL

This is one of the best ways to keep you on track with your zombie survival plans. Set yourself some achievable objectives and make an effort to do something 'zombie' every day – be it exercise, learning or checking your supplies.

▶ Start with scheduling an exercise programme and then noting your times and achievements each day.
▶ Arrange to stock up with a few extra items on shopping day and track your supplies.
▶ Schedule a weapons training hour every week and stick to it. Give yourself a reward if you complete five sessions.
▶ Ensure that you have a time each week when you revisit your survival plan. It may be daunting at the start, but pick up tasks every week and keep working through them.

ANTI-ZOMBIE PRODUCTS

There has been an explosion in the range of products on the market which profess to either 'cure' the zombic condition or 'scare' off the walking dead. The Ministry of Zombies, working with *What! Magazine,* has investigated many of these products and most have proven ineffective at best, and dangerous at worst.

To date, these investigations have ensured that over 300 products were removed from public sale. The most high-profile product taken off the virtual shelf being the now notorious range of Banjo Brand anti-ghoul merchandise, which flooded the market in 2009 and included all manner of creams, potions and tonics professing to help the unwary defend themselves against the dead. However, the battle goes on and new products seem to be emerging every week.

The market for anti-zombie products is not regulated by any international body as the items fall outside legislation on medicines for human usage and standard consumer products. Here are the worst offenders.

▶ MONROE'S ZOMBIE PELLETS

Simply spread the small brown pellets around your property, adding more as required at any point where the dead gather. The creatures will be drawn by the meaty scent of the pellets and consume them. But at Monroe's, we care too much to hurt these misguided souls. Once they have consumed our pellets, the dead will drift away – their desire for living flesh gone. A humane solution to a human problem.

'A SAFE AND HUMANE WAY TO ENSURE YOUR HOME STAYS FREE OF THE DEAD.'

PRODUCT REVIEW 👍

An expensive and useless product. We found these pellets to be a mixture of sawdust and glue. They have no effect on the dead but did attract significant numbers of slugs and snails. In addition, cats and dogs seem to find these dry pellets irresistible and suffer from the unpleasant side effect of acute trapped wind.

▶ BITE-AWAY

Using the latest research, Bite-Away cream will cure bites and scratches from any of the infected. Apply liberally to the affected area, slowly massaging the cooling cream into the wound. Within hours, the healing process will begin and you will be completely virus-free within 24 hours. If dizziness or moaning occurs, this may be a side effect or you could be turning into a zombie. Please consult your medical professional before use.

'THE WORLD'S FIRST ANTI-BACTERIAL VIRUS CREAM SPECIALLY FORMULATED TO HEAL THOSE IRRITATING ZOMBIE BITES!'

PRODUCT REVIEW 👍

This is a scandalous product, which is sold on multiple sites across the internet. Tests have shown that it contains no active ingredients and derives from cream for treating piles. Don't trust it, don't buy it. If you get bitten and use it, then you deserve what you get – you have been warned!

UNCLE TED'S ANTI-GHOUL TONIC

'SOMETIMES THE OLD WAYS ARE THE BEST AND OLD UNCLE TED KNEW HIS TONIC COULD REALLY CURE WHAT AILS YOU, SO WE JUST HAD TO GET IT TO YOU GOOD PEOPLE!'

Back in the old days Uncle Ted discovered the secret to curing the blight that brings the dead back to life. If you are feasted on by one of these unfortunates, take three table spoons of this powerful tonic and you'll wake up the next day feeling fine and dandy. Uncle Ted's Anti-Ghoul Tonic has been curing the undead for almost one hundred years. It is also available in a gallon spray can, which you can shower in.

BANJO BRAND

Banjo Brand products are notorious in the zombie fighting community for their ineffectiveness. The family making the range, which includes the dangerous Hi-Strength Healing Poultice said to 'cure' zombie bites, frequently moves between trailer parks across the United States and has so far eluded any state prosecution.

PRODUCT REVIEW 👍

This product has been on the market for decades and is a useless 'Hill Billy folksie' load of rubbish. Tests in the Ministry laboratories showed that it was at least 12% cat's urine and contained dangerous levels of lead and alcohol. Steer clear of the Banjo Brand and any of their products.

ZOMBIE-PROOF BODY SUIT

Developed by the US Government during the Cold War, Desiree Survival Fashions now brings you the world's first complete zombie-proof range of street wear. As others cower indoors, you'll be able to wander the streets, checking out the latest fashions in safety and the dead will ignore you as if you weren't there. Available in satin white, luscious peach and new naughty pink, a Micranax suit could be what you are looking for to ensure that just because the world's going to hell, it doesn't mean your sense of fashion has to as well!

'STYLISH PROTECTION AGAINST THE WALKING DEAD IN AN OUTFIT WHICH COMBINES CATWALK FASHION WITH A NON-EATABILITY INDEX OF OVER 90%.'

PRODUCT REVIEW 👍

We have no words to explain how poor this suit is. It is totally ineffective at protecting against the dead and retails on eBay at over £400. It appears to be a standard bee keeper's outfit with some glitter thrown on. We wonder what kind of fool would actually go for an obvious fake like this.

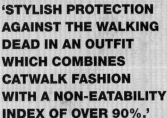

BECOMING A ZOMBIE SURVIVALIST

BUILD YOUR OWN SURVIVOR TEAM

Zombie survival is all about planning, so use the chart below to help assemble a team with the right skills to stay alive when the world goes to hell. If you don't know people who fit into these roles, get out there and meet them.

The Ministry of Zombies recognises ten distinct survival profiles which should be covered to give any group the best chance of survival. Of course, some skill sets may be covered by one individual, such as a skilful mechanic who is also adept at battling the dead. However, ensure that key skills are spread across the group. For example, everyone

will need to be able to wield a hand weapon and it will be useful if the whole team can pitch in making your home base safe. So, if necessary, audit the skills of your group and arrange training sessions to develop the skills you will need to survive. Don't panic if you don't have everything covered, but do take the time to work on any gaps.

As a final note on roles, it may be a good idea not to tell the person you have labelled 'first to die' as it may impact on their morale and ironically end up getting them killed sooner than they would otherwise have been.

TEAM LEADER

This is your role – make sure you are up to it. Start acting the part now by strutting around making 'firm but fair' decisions. With the knowledge gained from this volume, you will quickly become the 'go to' person.

GROUP MASCOT

Must be cute, chirpy and ready with a motivational phrase at all times including 'come on guys, there are only a few hundred' or 'if anything, it'll be more fun without ammunition'.

WEAPONS EXPERT

Armed with a baseball bat or crowbar, this fighter should love dealing with the dead up close and personal. They will also be responsible for ensuring that everyone else is armed and ready for combat.

THE MEDIC

A qualified doctor or nurse with the skills and first aid kit to complete everything from treating a strange rash to major surgery. Must come equipped with own plasters.

QUARTER -MASTER

This must be someone with an eye for detail and scrupulous honesty as they'll be managing the supplies. It'd be handy if they dislike many types of food as that way, your tins of peaches will be safe.

DIY GUY OR GAL

Carpentry, welding or bricklaying – this survivor must have all the skills crucial to keep your home fortress maintained. They should ideally have their own tools.

Creating a zombie neighbourhood watch group is a great way to protect your local area against the walking dead. Like a regular neighbourhood watch group it will involve meetings, agreeing a rota of patrols and communicating with your local law enforcement agencies.

You can begin the process with a friendly letter to all of your neighbours. It is often useful to include the phrase 'Have you ever worried about how you would cope if the zombies attacked our quiet road?' You'll be surprised how many people haven't given it a lot of thought.

Set a date for a 'kick off' meeting and start getting organised. On the agenda should be an audit of the skills you have within the group, a discussion of your defensive plans as well as an educational session using the content from this volume. Feel free to photocopy the pages you need for any neighbourhood watch work. Finally, it may be an idea to produce anti-zombie hats and stickers to help give a community feel to the whole venture. You can then sit back and watch the price of local homes soar as word gets out that your neighbourhood is 'zombie prepared'.

MECHANIC GUY OR GAL

You'll always need one of these to ensure that your post-apocalyptic wheels are kept running. Ideally, they should get along with your DIY person as they will often have to team up. Select someone who comes with their own tools.

EX-SPECIAL FORCES

It is always useful to have your own armed and trained killer. This survivor will become your right hand and you need to be able to rely on them to report back on any potential trouble within the group. You may even end up needing them to 'solve a problem' for you.

FIRST TO DIE

A tough slot to fill but if the old series of *Star Trek* taught us anything, it is that you must always have one of those guys in the red security shirts as they invariably die first. Do not reveal to this person that they fulfil this role.

DAZED AND CONFUSED

There must alway be someone in your group who is in a state of denial about the dead or raving on the edge about the 'world that's gone'. They will use phrases such as 'we're all gonna die!' and 'game over man, game over!'.

GROUP LAWYER

It is important to always have adequate legal representation – only joking. Leave them outside. Some professions which demand vast salaries now will be worthless in the world of the zombies. It's very sad but true.

HOME PREPARATION AND DEFENCE

It is not uncommon for readers taking zombies seriously for the first time to have that 'light bulb' moment when they realise that the walking dead are a real threat to our way of life and that without some serious preparation, things are going to get ugly very quickly.

Before even looking at your own zombie preparation plans, it is important to understand the key principles of home defence against the dead.

In previous chapters, we have learnt about how zombies are created, their abilities and behaviour and it's upon this information that any zombie defence should be based. It is important to grasp how remorseless these creatures are. They may not win any prizes in general intelligence, but they will claw, scratch and push their way into the homes of many of the unprepared. It shocks many new to zombie survival to discover that one of the safest places to be during a zombie apocalypse is actually in the comfort of your own home. Imagine the chaos out on the streets as the dead mix freely with the living and confusion abounds? Wouldn't you rather be tucked up safely in your own zombie-proof home? The following pages will provide you with knowledge and skills not only to stay safe in the home but also to survive for more than 90 days in a home cut off from the world.

ZOMBIE PROOFING DIY

It is not uncommon for trainee zombie survivalists to start looking around their home and quickly become overwhelmed by the sheer number of jobs which require attention. For example, should we have built a six-foot brick wall instead of that rockery or would the money paid for laying a new lawn have been better spent on setting punji stake pits along the drive. However, do not panic! The Ministry of Zombies has created a complete home audit system which you can use to assess your home in its current condition and develop a realistic plan to start addressing the key areas of zombie defence weakness. Remember, not everything needs to be done at once, and many of the improvements are low cost.

However, before completing a home audit you should learn the basics of zombie home defence. This simple model was laid down in the 1990s and is known in the wider zombie-fighting community as the 'Principles of Zombie Home Defence'. In a nutshell, these principles recommend three lines of defence against the dead for any dwelling.

HOME PREPARATION AND DEFENCE
SAFEST PLACES TO BE DURING A ZOMBIE APOCALYPSE

The Ministry of Zombies asked 1000 members of the public where they thought the safest place would be during a zombie apocalypse.

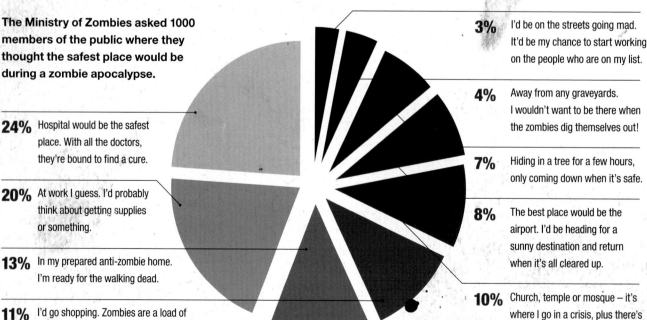

24% Hospital would be the safest place. With all the doctors, they're bound to find a cure.

20% At work I guess. I'd probably think about getting supplies or something.

13% In my prepared anti-zombie home. I'm ready for the walking dead.

11% I'd go shopping. Zombies are a load of rubbish so why miss out on some bargains?

3% I'd be on the streets going mad. It'd be my chance to start working on the people who are on my list.

4% Away from any graveyards. I wouldn't want to be there when the zombies dig themselves out!

7% Hiding in a tree for a few hours, only coming down when it's safe.

8% The best place would be the airport. I'd be heading for a sunny destination and return when it's all cleared up.

10% Church, temple or mosque – it's where I go in a crisis, plus there's always a good buffet on the go.

SURVEY VERIFIED BY THE MARKET INSIGHT GROUP

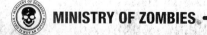

▶ PRINCIPLES OF ZOMBIE HOME DEFENCE

1ST PRINCIPLE
EXTERNAL PERIMETER

The first principle of any defence against the dead is to have a robust external perimeter. In most cases, this will be a garden fence or wall, but equally the same principles would apply if you were defending a shop, a police station or any building. The external perimeter is your first line of defence and if breached should enable you to fall back in good order.

2ND PRINCIPLE
INTERIOR PERIMETER

The second principle of defence against the dead is to have a 'zombie proof' interior perimeter. In reality, no location or defensive line can ever be 100% zombie proof – the dead will always find a way in eventually. However, in a typical residential scenario this interior perimeter should include double-glazed or barred windows and strong doors. If the horde breaks through your first line, you should be able to slam that front door and be safe from the zombies as you regroup. Within your interior perimeter is the so-called 'green zone' where any living quarters will be. Survivors can normally move around this area unarmed.

EXTERNAL PERIMETER
GARDEN FENCE OR WALL

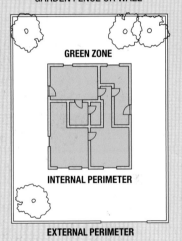

EXTERNAL PERIMETER

INTERNAL PERIMETER
WALLS, WINDOWS AND DOORS

INTERNAL PERIMETER

SAFE ROOM
FALL-BACK POSITION

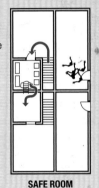

The stairs are raised and the family rush to the safe room

The zombies burst in and ground floor is overrun

SAFE ROOM

3RD PRINCIPLE
FINAL LINE OF DEFENCE

The third principle of zombie defence is the creation of a final line of defence or a 'safe room'. This is your ultimate fallback position if your home is overrun. In this scenario, survivors typically have very little time to plan, perhaps the dead have forced a door open or someone has accidentally let them through a window. Whatever the cause, the impact is akin to a tidal wave of rotting ghouls flooding into the house. You and your group therefore need a location which is secure, to re-group again and plan your next move. The safe room does not actually need to be a room – many survivors remove ground-floor stairs so they can cut off their upper floors if required. Any safe room must have basic supplies, strong doors and any essentials you feel necessary for a break out. Many survivors create escape routes through the ceiling of safe rooms – possibly moving into the next house through the loft. In the early days of the apocalypse, you and your group may sleep sealed in the safe room for extra security, but do not forget you should always have a guard on duty.

⚠ WARNING

UNLIKE MANY OF THE PRE-BUILT COMMERCIALLY AVAILABLE SAFE ROOMS ON THE MARKET TODAY, A ZOMBIE SAFE ROOM IS NOT A LOCATION TO LOCK YOURSELF IN UNTIL HELP ARRIVES. IF YOU LOCK YOURSELF IN A REGULAR SAFE ROOM AS THE DEAD PILE UP AGAINST THE DOOR, IT COULD BECOME YOUR TOMB AS YOU WILL BE UNABLE TO ESCAPE AND THIS TIME, HELP CERTAINLY WON'T BE COMING! A ZOMBIE SAFE ROOM MUST ALWAYS HAVE AN ALTERNATIVE EXIT...

THE ZOMBIE HOME PREPARATION AUDIT

The home survey opposite was developed in conjunction with the Home Builders Association of America, the British Building Standards Group and the Irish Institute of Construction. You should print a copy and try to approach your home with 'fresh eyes'. It is important to get inside the mind of a zombie and imagine their attack points. Try wearing a yellow safety hat and use a clip board when you are completing the work to give you that 'official' look.

Walk methodically around your home 'scoring' against the various criteria on the form. If necessary, hire an expert to complete the survey. A completed Zombie Home Preparation Audit is the place the start in zombie home defence, regardless of the score.

HOW IT WORKS

Each home or location starts with 100 points and points are deducted for each risk assessed. You can improve your home score over time by mitigating a risk. We have included some examples, but feel free to deduct more points for any other extra hazards. Be harsh with your scoring.

Complete the form, but do not be alarmed if the results are poor at first. If you score zero in some categories you may wish to move on. For example, if you are next to a hospital or in an unsuitable rented property then consider moving immediately.

On completing this assessment, your first action should be to prioritise a list of measures to improve any future assessment. Remember that you should not start spending serious money on bulking items such as underground water storage tanks while forgetting about areas such as double-glazing and essential roof repairs. Get the basics right first then develop your property.

Final note on home defence: it's not all about the zombies. With the zombie apocalypse will come armies of looters and unmentionables. So, if you are sitting in a superb zombie fortification that everyone knows about, be prepared for them paying you a visit. It may be worth making any improvements in secret and even giving your home that 'worn out' look to fool any would-be human attackers.

They say there's 'no place like home' and if you get your preparation right, you will have made a major step towards surviving the zombies so approach the whole audit process seriously and with the knowledge that detailed and critical observation now could prevent one of your loved ones becoming a snack for the ghouls.

ANALYSING THE RESULTS

Originally, the Zombie Home Preparation Audit was meant to be completed by trained professionals to form part of a Home Information Pack whenever a residence is sold or let, but changes in government policy in both the USA and UK have meant that you now need to complete this work yourself. The information below offers some general advice based on your score. Remember, these are generic guidelines as every home is different.

If one 'area of investigation' scores zero and there is no practical way to mitigate the risk then consider moving as soon as possible. For example, you may live next door to a high-risk site or a prime looting location, in which case, it's time to start packing.

LESS THAN 40

You and your family are in serious danger of being a cheap meat snack the moment the dead arrive. There are just too many holes in your zombie defences. If you can't improve the situation, move.

40 TO 60

A reasonable score for a first assessment but where you have identified areas of improvement, make those changes now. For example, the kids may be unhappy now when you brick up their bedroom window, but they'll be pleased later when they can play in peace with the zombies stuck outside.

61 TO 80

A great start. Either you have made some improvements already or you have bought or rented a property very wisely. Build on your current defences and keep it up. You have a good chance of surviving the initial chaos so keep going and always look for ways to take things to the next level. For example, could you convert that rockery into an M-60 machine gun pit? It's just a suggestion.

81 TO 100

You've given yourself a real chance of survival, but are there any small improvements you could make? Equally, always be careful that your home is not too obvious in its defences. If you run around the neighbourhood boasting of the zombie robustness of your home – guess where everyone is going to head for when the chaos starts? Any secure home fortress that is too obvious will be an advert to every desperate survivor out there who won't think twice about scooting in there while you are in the garden and locking you out.

AREA OF INVESTIGATION	HAZARDS TO BE ASSESSED	SCORE
Exterior Hazards and Environs — The site location and surrounding area	▶ Close to hospital, place of worship etc. ▶ Close proximity to 'looting' location. ▶ No access to clean water source. ▶ Telegraph pole or tree nearby.	/10
Property Visual Inspection — How well maintained the property is in general	▶ Poorly maintained building. ▶ Only one access point. ▶ No chimney or open fire. ▶ Poorly maintained roof/broken tiles.	/10
Outer Perimeter — The robustness of the external perimeter such as the property boundary or exterior fencing	▶ No secure outside garden. ▶ No secure outside buildings. ▶ Inadequate exterior fencing.	/20
Inner Perimeter — The robustness of the internal perimeter such as windows, doors and any other access points	▶ No double-glazing. ▶ Poorly fitted doors or rotting frames. ▶ Small, unbarred low windows.	/20
Safe Room Potential — Assessing the property's capabilities if zombies break in	▶ Single storey. ▶ Weak interior doors. ▶ Poor internal layout with too many 'dead ends'.	/10
Self-sufficiency Potential — Comfort and resources over the medium to long term	▶ Poor storage potential. ▶ No secure basement. ▶ No secure outside space. ▶ Limited water storage.	/20
Zombie Attack Role Play — A freestyle role play attack, highlighting any weak points	▶ Zombies' ability to gain access. ▶ Zombies collapsing an exterior fence. ▶ Zombies forcing open a garage door. ▶ Zombies managing to reach through poorly secured window.	/10

TOTAL SCORE   OUT OF 100

HOME PREPARATION AND DEFENCE

TOP HOME REPAIR TIPS

Defending against the zombies starts with the basics. It's pointless spending a fortune on the ultimate zombie safe room if your home is poorly insulated, the roof is in danger of collapsing or the front door is coming off its hinges.

Looking at all the areas that require attention can easily overwhelm the new zombie survivalist so the Ministry of Zombies has created a simple six-step process to creating a safer home. It may surprise people to find that steps such as gaining invaluable DIY skills and insulating your home come before smashing up the stairs. Use a completed zombie home preparation audit along with these six key pointers to get yourself and your house ready for a major zombie outbreak and remember, not everything will be about buying more planks of wood.

1 YOUR OWN DIY SKILLS

Every zombie survivalist should also be a do-it-yourself expert. You won't be able to call a plumber during the zombie apocalypse so learn the basics now. The same goes for carpentry and basic building work. Get on as many courses as you can and ensure you have the right tools. The better you know your household, the more you will be able to rely on your skills to defend it when you have to.

2 WALL AND LOFT INSULATION

It makes sense to ensure that your home is as insulated as possible to protect you and your family in the cold months ahead. So, this includes wall and loft insulation. The zombie survivalist should also explore solar panels, wind generators and reliable diesel generators for when the power goes down. Get an Energy Performance Certificate commissioned if you are unsure of what to do.

3 WINDOWS AND DOORS

Double glazing is a cost-effective improvement to any home but will pay dividends once the electricity goes off and you are left with little heating. In addition, zombies cannot break through such windows. Consider triple-glazing if you can and then the option of adding bars or a steel rolling blind. Pay particular attention to door frames as they are often overlooked – it is pointless having a strong door only to have it cave in under the pressure of the zombies due to a poorly fitted frame!

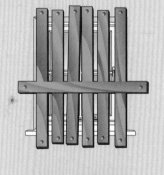

1 Hammer planks over the windows then place a support across. 40% of all zombie break-ins are through open windows – so back them!

2 A basic support will strengthen any door. It only works on doors that open inwards.

A wedged bar at the bottom of the stairs will also work.

4 FIX THAT LEAKY ROOF

Never forget to regularly inspect and repair this crucial part of your home. Any leaks when you are surrounded by the dead could quickly become major problems so get them sorted now. More than one zombie siege in history has ended due to supplies being flooded via a leaky roof. Also check your guttering and exterior drains as well as any other flood risks.

5 CREATING A SAFE ROOM

Every zombie survivalist home should have a 'safe room' – a strongly fortified fallback position to which everyone will run if your perimeter is compromised. In most homes, the easiest way to do this is to convert any stairs into a drawbridge style defence which will allow you to seal off the upper floors. If you are in a single-storey dwelling then convert one room into a safe room by reinforcing the interior door and making space for your Bug-Out Bags.

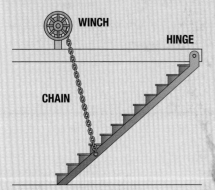

WINCH

HINGE

CHAIN

1 It is a good idea to hire a professional carpenter to create your 'drawbridge stairs' as the workings should be robust and, ideally, the fittings flush.

WINCH RAISES THE STAIRS

2 At night or during any breach, once all the survivors have scampered up the stairs, you can raise the drawbridge and effectively seal off the lower floor.

6 STRENGTHENING AN EXTERIOR FENCE

You must ensure your perimeter is well defended. A horde of zombies can put incredible pressure on your fence – most of it is lateral pressure. If you have the resources then consider fitting a reinforced deep sunk steel fence as outside space will be invaluable during any zombie siege.

1 Surveying your fence, look out for any weak spots including fence posts.

2 Dig in some lateral supports to start with. Focus on fence posts and then other sections.

3 Prepare some pre-mixed concrete, paying careful attention to the water ratios. 2–3 minutes of mixing will be required.

PRE-MIX CEMENT

4 Carefully excavate the fence foundations. Distract the zombies when strengthening the foundations with concrete. Do the same for the lateral support.

5 You may want to create a basic 'firestep'. You may now fire at the dead safe in the knowledge that your humble garden fence has been well and truly 'pimped'!

HOME PREPARATION AND DEFENCE

THE PERFECT ANTI-ZOMBIE HOME

Whether you stayed tucked away in a fortified and isolated log cabin in the woods or stuck in a grimy apartment on the outskirts of a major town, no one location is 100% zombie proof. But in 2009, architects Foster & Webber Associates was commissioned to draw up plans for the world's first affordable anti-zombie family dwelling. A budget of $500,000 was allocated for the new build and although the project did end up costing more, it was never meant to be a fantasy home, with underground bunkers and so on. It was designed as

the prototype for mass-produced homes of the future. Homes which have the added attraction of being zombie resistant, as they are referred to, and this was no flight of fancy; several major house builders who funded the project were responding to data published in the *Property and Real Estate Journal* which indicated that over 63% of home buyers took zombie defence potential into consideration and that for 5% of people, it was the most important consideration in the purchase.

▶ ZOMBIE-RESISTANT HOME

For the ultimate zombie 'prepper', building your home purposely designed to resist the walking dead is the obvious choice, but cost should not be the only consideration. Choosing the right location is also key. Select a building plot too close to, say, a hospital or an army base and you may be overrun despite all of your preparations.

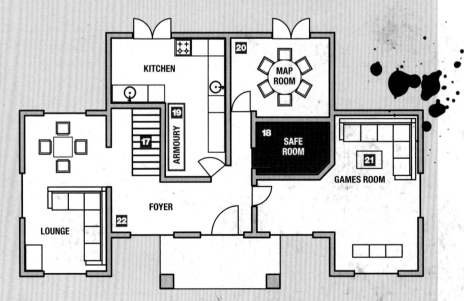

1 Solid external perimeter fence with lateral supports to resist pressure.

2 Razor wire on top of fence.

3 'Green zone' of safety behind the fence.

4 Vegetable patches.

5 A dug well for extra water.

6 Secure exit and access for vehicles.

7 All windows triple glazing.

8 All lower windows barred.

9 Solid doors to access ground floor.

10 Lookout location from top of house.

11 Heavily insulated roof for cold weather.

12 Chimney and open fires in most rooms.

13 Ample storage space in basement, including sizeable water tank.

14 Rain collection tanks on roof to provide water for washing.

15 Solar panels and wind generators.

16 Emergency diesel generator.

17 Stairs can be lifted to seal off upper floors.

18 Heavily fortified safe room.

19 Secure armoury of weapons.

20 Map room – showing foraging locations.

21 Games room for recreation.

22 Bug-Out Bags checked and ready to go at a moment's notice.

KITCHEN

20 MAP ROOM

19 ARMOURY

17

18 SAFE ROOM

21 GAMES ROOM

FOYER

22

LOUNGE

FOSTER & WEBBER ASSOCIATES

PROJECT COST:	£1.2m per unit
BUILD TIME:	Two months
ARCHITECTS:	Foster & Webber

HOME PREPARATION AND DEFENCE
BUYING A NEW HOME

People buying new homes are already beginning to make zombie-defence criteria part of their buying decision. A recent survey revealed that 5% of purchasers see good zombie defence as 'very important', representing a 50% increase on the same survey two years ago.

31% LOCATION
What is the neighbourhood like?

15% CONDITION
Is the property well maintained?

14% BEDROOMS
How many bedrooms are there?

2% FAMILY
Is it close to friends and family?

3% TRANSPORT
Where is the nearest bus stop?

5% ZOMBIES
Is this property easily defended against zombies?

8% AMENITIES
How close are the shops, gym?

10% SCHOOLS
How good are the local schools?

12% PARKING
Has it got off-street parking?

SURVEY OF 10,023 PURCHASERS ACROSS THE USA, UK AND GERMANY IN AUGUST 2011

HOME PREPARATION AND DEFENCE

90-DAY RATIONS

A central pillar of the 90-day survival plan is having enough supplies to survive in isolation from the world for the entire period. There is a chance that you could forage an abandoned home after a few weeks, but you should exercise frugality to be self-sufficient in your home fortress in terms of food, water and other supplies.

As a zombie survivalist, you need to start asking some searching questions about your current set-up such as how much food do I currently keep in the house? Do I have a good place to store supplies and, most importantly, do I really think I could last for a few months on one carton of orange juice and a box of cornflakes? More than any part of the 90-day survival plan, laying down stores requires planning and ongoing management. Most items will need to be rotated according to date and you'll need a dry, dark and cool place to store most food items.

Remember to personalise your supplies. If you hate tinned peas then there is no reason to see out the apocalypse almost spewing every time you force them down. Stock what you enjoy within the main food groups and adjust your stock to take into account any special dietary requirements.

▶ FOOD SUPPLIES

The key in food storage is planning. Firstly, consider the number of survivors you are likely to have, then map out a 3–4 month period of isolation. Secondly, plan the main meal for each day per person. Be conservative with portions and keep a balanced diet for an active person. Don't forget to include treats and to mix things up or there is a risk that after the third straight week of watery gruel, your fellow survivors may be willingly walking into the arms of the hungry dead just to escape your cooking.

EMERGENCY FOOD SUPPLIES

The following items are suggested when selecting emergency food supplies. You may already have many of these to hand.

▶ Ready-to-eat canned meats, fruits, vegetables and a can opener – fresh vegetables will be hard to come by as the distribution network collapses and will be a welcome treat.
▶ Protein or fruit bars will often replace a lunchtime meal. After a busy afternoon bashing zombies, you'll need a snack.
▶ Dried milk powder – the miracle substance and heart of a thousand survival recipes. Ensure you have ample supplies.
▶ Peanut butter packed with the power of this glorious nut, is a great snack on dried biscuits.
▶ Dried fruit – will keep much longer than fresh fruit. Just look at those dried dates you got from an Auntie a few years ago – they're still as delicious now as the day you were given them.
▶ Crackers – a great way to boost up any meal and perfect for snacks.
▶ Canned juices – again, you will need these to ensure a balanced diet.
▶ Food for infants – don't forget if you have little ones or anyone requiring a special diet, you need to plan for this.

Some survival supplies offer a complete 90-day food supply and they range from around £600 per person. You may also opt for dried military rations if you really want to be hardcore.

HOME PREPARATION AND DEFENCE
SELF-SUFFICIENT LIVING

Self-sufficiency living is not just about big-time gardening, it's a whole approach and something you can start implementing immediately. The first step is to identify the key 'inputs' into your home – so we are talking about fruit, vegetables, meat, fish, water etc. Basically, everything you can currently just go to the supermarket for and top up whenever you please. Self-sufficiency living is about gradually reducing your dependency on these external sources. For example, is there a nearby field with a secure fence which may be suitable for larger scale gardening? Do you have space for a greenhouse which could guarantee you fresh produce all year round and

do you have the necessary skills to catch wild animals such as rabbits to supplement your meat intake? Work to gradually develop your level of self-sufficiency now in preparation for the zombie apocalypse and it won't be such a shock when the dead arrive. Try to build a library of information in areas such as gardening and the smallholder management of livestock. The possibility of catching fish from a nearby river or lake is tempting but depends very much on the number of bodies floating in the water. Most zombie experts expect main waterways to be blocked with the bloated corpses of the dead so you may want to hold the fish for the moment!

FOODS THAT LAST

Here's a handy list of foods that can be stored for over 3 years in the right containers and conditions:

- ▶ Wheat.
- ▶ Vegetable oil.
- ▶ Corn.
- ▶ Baking powder (you can never have enough).
- ▶ Soya beans.
- ▶ Instant coffee, tea.
- ▶ Cocoa (this is a must have).
- ▶ Salt.
- ▶ Non-carbonated soft drinks.
- ▶ White rice.
- ▶ Dry pasta.
- ▶ Powdered milk (in nitrogen-packed cans) – an essential.
- ▶ Apparently, baked beans in a tin can last over 15 years. We're not sure whether this is a comfort or not.
- ▶ Honey and sugar if correctly stored will last for years and liven up many a dull survival meal.
- ▶ Dried apple slices may not sound like much of a treat now but they'll last for years.
- ▶ Dehydrated carrots aren't the tastiest but they do the job.

REMEMBER THE KEY TO KEEPING FOOD IS STORING IT IN THE CORRECT CONDITIONS AND ROTATING YOUR STOCKS!

A FINAL NOTE

Do not be disheartened if you currently have low stocks. Most people today shop on an almost daily basis and are quite used to picking what they want, whenever they want it at the drop of a hat. Start to change your mindset now and build your food stocks up slowly if funds are tight. Create your vegetable patch now and start practising your survival recipes right away. Any sudden change in diet can be a serious shock to your body – imagine moving your survivor group onto your cabbage-based survival diet only to be driven out of your sealed fortress by the mixture of a non-functioning toilet and the unpleasant vapours from your fellow survivors.

HOME PREPARATION AND DEFENCE

▶ WATER

To be on the safe side, you should allocate one gallon of clean water per adult per day. In purely survival terms, this is generous and other factors such as climate and level of activity will play a part. The 'one gallon a day' calculation includes a small allocation for washing and sanitation. It is important that you should never let your water supply drop below a three-day supply per person in your group.

KEY POINTS ABOUT WATER

1 Commercial firms can provide tanks of over 2000 gallons if you are serious about securing your supply.

2 Rainwater can be collected for washing or sanitation, but be cautious of water from a stream – always boil it and use a purifier, particularly if it smells a bit 'corpsy'.

3 There is a reservoir of water in the heating system and tanks in most homes – make sure you trap it.

4 When things kick off, run and fill every bath you have in the house – this can provide a useful reserve.

5 Maintain strict water-usage discipline at all times.

5 REASONS WHY SURVIVORS VENTURE INTO ZOMBIETOWN

Any journey into bandit country will be dangerous, but figures collected by the Ministry of Zombies reveal the top five reasons why survivors leave their fortified homes during zombie outbreaks. These findings were based on research into more than 100 documented incidents since 1946.

1 We ran out of water so I went to forage.

2 Food was low and I wanted a bit of variety.

3 I was feeling claustrophobic.

4 I couldn't stand being trapped with those people any longer.

5 I just fancied getting some fresh air.

Apart from the fact that some of these responses are sheer lunacy, running out of water is the number one reason why survivors leave the safety of their shelter and put themselves at risk on the zombie-dominated streets. Clearly, this shows that most survivors seriously underestimated their requirements in terms of water.

OTHER SUPPLIES

Preparing a 90-day survival plan will take time and resources, and when you are on a limited budget it makes sense to concentrate on home fortification, food and water as the priorities. In addition, it's always worth putting a small budget aside for other items – not just the crucial stuff like tools, extra wood, nails and any medicines but also books, games and those little luxuries that make life worth living.

If there are children in the house, consider how you are going to keep them entertained during those long dreary nights – perhaps a collection of classic children's books and toys. Once your e-reader packs up, you'll be back to good old paperbacks so keep a good stock as they can also be useful as kindling for a fire. You can use your powerless e-reader to put plants on, or as a small chopping board.

In addition to these, start building up a library of survival textbooks now – knowledge of first aid, growing your own crops and basic mechanics will become invaluable. It may be an idea to create a 'planning room' in your home where you can store all your books and plans. If you've always wanted one of those rooms you see on TV shows, with photos pinned to the wall and bits of blue string joining things up – this is your chance. Get your survival plans organised and use the planning room for meetings with your survival team. It will help to create the air of seriousness required among the group and make you look like an expert or lunatic depending on the observer.

'DON'T FORGET' ITEMS

Here's a quick 'don't forget' list of essentials put together by a team of survival experts – these are items people typically forget:

▶ **WIND-UP RADIO**

To keep updated with any emergency broadcasts.

▶ **TOILET PAPER**

You'll thank us for this one.

▶ **SHAMPOO**

You can battle the dead and still have coconut fresh hair.

▶ **FIRST AID BOX**

Well-stocked. Check dates on the tablets.

▶ **EXTRA BLANKETS**

For when the heating is out.

▶ **GARBAGE BAGS**

You can never have enough of these.

▶ **MATCHES**

Loads of matches.

▶ **AN ENTERTAINMENT BOX FOR THE KIDS**

Including crap board games with pieces missing and old children's books that will put the zombies to sleep.

▶ **ANOTHER BLANKET**

Someone spilt something on the first one.

▶ **WIND-UP TORCH**

These cheap items could be a life saver if you find yourself needing light in an emergency. They aren't very bright but they do the job.

▶ POWER

WHAT HAPPENS WHEN THE LIGHTS GO OUT?

Few people in the developed world live without some form of power in their home and one thing you can be sure of is that once the zombies are in town, it's only a matter of time before the power grid goes down. Survival experts disagree on how long it will last in the aftermath of the apocalypse so it's best to plan for it being out from day one. Invest in a basic portable generator and lay down enough fuel to last you at least a few months. A small generator on average will use about a gallon a day if used continuously. Below is a list of items you can power with a portable generator (5000 watts per hour)

▶ Central air-conditioning (5000 watts).
▶ X-Box (200 watts).
▶ Standard TV (190 watts).
▶ Computer (120 watts).
▶ Monitor (150 watts).
▶ Laptop (200 watts).
▶ Hot plate (1200 watts).
▶ Oven (3000 watts).
▶ Popcorn popper (1,600 watts).
▶ Average lightbulb (25 watts).
▶ Your illuminated Captain Kirk water feature diorama (7,500 watts of wasted energy).

Obviously, you can't have everything on at once so budget your energy provisions carefully. In addition, a well-lit house amid the darkness will be an open invitation to any bandit out there that you are well supplied and comfortable – expect a visit from your local looters just as your popcorn is popping in the maker. No one knows exactly how long the power will stay on when the dead rise. Research has shown that many of our power stations, including the nuclear ones, can continue for weeks unmanned before auto shutting down. As part of your survival preparations, it is prudent to have several practice weekends without power to really grasp the impact it has on a survival group.

COPING WITH DISABILITIES

The streets being dominated by thousands of ravenous corpses will present challenges to everyone but those with disabilities need additional planning to ensure they are in a position to defend themselves and help others when the dead arrive.

For example, if you have serious mobility problems then it may be useful to extend the 90-day survival plan into a 120-day plan by stocking up on additional food and supplies. Weapons, bags and other locations will all need to be adapted to take any disability into consideration.

There are also some very obvious challenges which need to be considered, for example, if you have limited mobility, how will you manage if all of the elevators fail or you are caught in a panicky crowd as the zombies attack? You should analyse your potential needs against some of the scenarios outlined in this survival manual. Plan for the worst case scenario and have a recommended action in each example.

CRISIS GUIDELINES FOR THOSE WITH DISABILITIES OR SPECIAL NEEDS

The Ministry of Zombies has worked with a number of emergency organisations to produce a basic plan to support your zombie planning and preparation. Many of these guidelines also apply to the elderly.

Remember, society is going to be an even tougher place as things fall apart so don't treat the zombie apocalypse as a regular crisis.

▶ **PLAN AHEAD OF ANY ZOMBIE CRISIS**
Ensure that your plan is documented and that any family and close friends are aware of the details.

▶ **IT'S ABOUT YOU**
You are in the best position to know about your own care – think carefully about what you'd do if the dead appeared before you had a chance to go into lockdown?

▶ **COMPLETE A PERSONAL NEEDS ASSESSMENT**
Similar to what you'd do in regular emergency planning. Ensure that it is based on your abilities after the crisis. Base your assessment of the conditions of a zombie apocalypse and at the lowest level of your abilities – play it safe.

▶ **CREATE A PERSONAL SUPPORT NETWORK**
These will be trusted and trained people you can rely on in a crisis. You may decide to turn your own home into a fortress and make it a gathering point for those in your network.

5 TIPS FOR PREPARING FOR THE ZOMBIES

31-year-old Gulf War veteran Steve Langdon is the official spokesmen for the Ministry of Zombies on zombie defence and disability.

1 Zombies don't care who you are, they'll eat you just as quickly. So no matter what disability you have, get educated and start training now.

2 Complete a bespoke audit of any health requirements as part of your preparation. If you require any medication, stock up now but manage the 'best before' dates carefully.

3 Choose an appropriate weapon. For wheelchair users like myself, a metal baseball bat works well but for others a lighter weapon may be more suitable. Remember, a crutch or a walking stick can easily be converted into an effective bashing weapon. Get creative!

4 Working with a network of trusted survivors is the best strategy so keep your own survival skills updated. Become an invaluable member of the team – learn about first aid, weapons care and home repair skills.

5 Don't be a victim. You gotta toughen up now before the zombies arrive. There will be gangs of desperate survivors out there ready to snatch your gear – be in a position to say 'just try it!' with a wicked grin on your face.

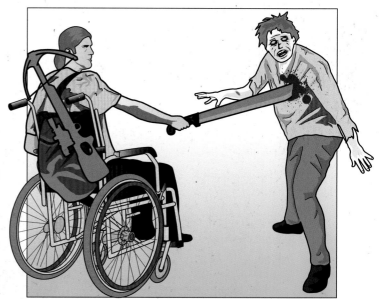

► STEVE LANGDON'S ZOMB-CHAIR

Whatever your disability, you need to start planning now for the day the zombies arrive. If you are partially sighted, think about a longer sweeping weapon to defend yourself with. If you have mobility problems, research now and make sure that you can still get around and 'do the business' with the zombies. Steve Langdon's California-based company Mobility Solutions has developed a post-apocalyptic prototype wheelchair known as the Zomb-Chair.

❝ IF THERE ARE ADULTS OR KIDS OUT THERE READING THIS WHO HAVE DISABILITIES, KNOW THIS – YOU GET YOURSELF PREPARED AND YOU'LL HAVE A BETTER CHANCE OF SURVIVAL THAN THOUSANDS OF OTHERS ❞
CAPTAIN STEVE 'RUSTY' LANGDON

To date, Langdon has created ten Zomb-Chairs for various clients around the world and is looking to scale up production, but with each chair costing at least $30,000, for the moment they are out of reach for most zombie survivalists. He plans to introduce a cheaper, scaled down version in the next few years and has already secured orders for Zomb-Chair 2 from survivors around the world.

1. Caterpillar tracks providing all-terrain capability.
2. Built-in shot gun which be easily stored on-board.
3. Batteries offering up to 50 hours of continuous use.
4. Manual recharger in case you need extra power.
5. Attached smoke bombs to create distractions and cover.
6. Machine gun (fixed) to take down any hordes.
7. Holder for melee weapon for close combat.
8. Bug-Out Bag storage area which may also be used for loot.
9. Antenna for communication with home base.
10. Defensive rear shield to protect from unseen attackers.
11. Steel tube frame construction.
12. Seat belts to maintain posture and firing position.
13. Retractable spikes from wheels for additional zombie-killing power.

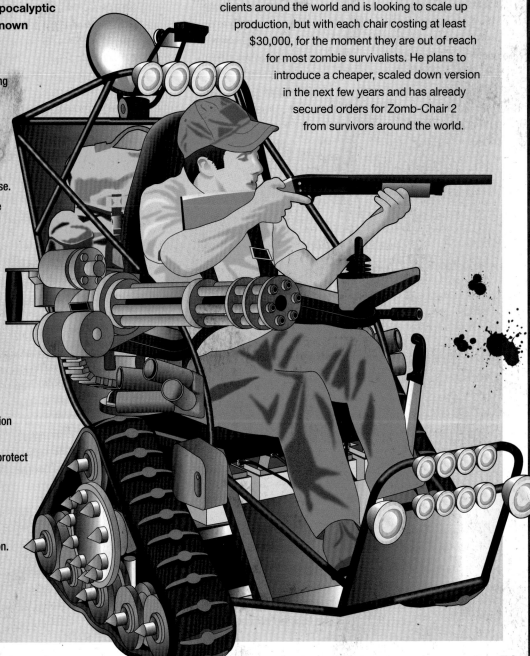

HOME PREPARATION AND DEFENCE

COPING WITH CHILDREN

For families, one of the most challenging tasks will be preparing children for the zombie apocalypse. Depending on their age, they may have some knowledge, but the 'monsters' outside the window will no doubt haunt most for years to come if you don't get that balance right. For example, do you reveal the ugly truth now so that they are pre-warned of the horrors ahead, or sugar-coat it and turn survival training into a fun adventure game? Child psychologists disagree on which approach is best, but simple activities such as keeping children entertained and allocating them small tasks around the home can be a great way to start. Ensure they are involved, keep them updated with developments and, with care, start to train them in the combat skills required to survive.

BUFFO COMIC

In the 1960s, the Ministry of Zombies in London embarked upon an innovative strategy to educate children on the danger of zombies. The comic book *Buffo* – which was published in the USA and the UK between 1963 and 1983, featured a whole series of educational cartoons. They were considered old-fashioned even at the time but were designed to be used by parents to introduce the threat of zombies and ensure that the children understood what to do if they saw one of the walking dead. We have included a favourite classic from 1968 in which an overzealous junior zombie spotter finally manages to stop a major zombie outbreak. You may want to photocopy these – the *Buffo* comics were big sellers in the zombie fighting community right up to when the comic was cancelled in 1983.

Anytown is a quiet suburb but amateur junior detective Annie Riggs is always on the lookout for zombies. This week she can't get out and about on her brand new red bicycle as she's been grounded by Mummy after the

She's looking out of the window

ANNIE: I can't go out & play today so I'll just sit here zombie spotting. I just know they'll be here today!

Gosh I'm bored as a bicycle. Hang on, what's that coming up the path?

Annie spots a stranger

ANNIE: Mother, it's a zombie! He's limping & everything!

MOTHER: No dear, that's the postman Frank. He got that limp during the war.

Soon another visitor approaches

ANNIE: Mother, it's a zombie. He's staggering all over the place!

MOTHER: No dear, that's Albert the gardener. He likes a half in The Kings Head before his afternoon rounds!

HOME PREPARATION AND DEFENCE
COPING WITH CHILDREN

CHILDREN AND ZOMBIES DO NOT MIX

The uninformed child can find the lumbering movements and unbalanced gait of zombies humorous and this can lead to serious consequences. Educate your children now. There are many great kids' books out on the market. We have included some classic cartoons from yesteryear.

ARM AS APPROPRIATE

Training is key when any weapons are involved, but your kids must be able to protect themselves. As a rule of thumb, if they are over 10 years old then they should receive a good level of hand weapons training. Younger children may be restricted to the safe areas of your home base. Remember, the world will have changed and your kids need the right skills to survive.

DON'T UNDERESTIMATE LITTLE ONES

Even young children are immensely adaptable and have proved so in countless zombie incidents. Don't overlook them or leave them locked inside if they are keen to contribute. If they are old enough to ask about the zombies then they have the right to know what's going on.

KEEP THINGS FUN

This could apply to everyone. Sure, it's the end of the world as we know it, but keep your child entertained with games, books and things to do. A humorous game of 'who can spot the funniest zombie' can help kill the hours during a zombie siege. Ensure that your supplies include plenty of creative things to do. It's boredom that will cause most problems so prepare now.

trouble she caused by reporting her elderly neighbours, Mr & Mrs Arkwright, for being Russian spies – turns out they were just going on holiday! The long school holidays are really beginning to drag for Annie and she can't wait to go out exploring again but soon her day is going to be interrupted by some rather queer strangers!

Annie is most unhappy

ANNIE: This is just not cricket. I just know the zombies are out there and I need to keep Anytown safe. I know – I'll get my Bumper Book of the Dead I got for Christmas!

Now in place with her book, she sees another figure staggering up the path.

Annie checks her book

ANNIE: Righto, staggering, yes, limping yes, blood thirsty look, yes. This has just got to be one, it just has to be! Mum! There's a zombie in the garden!

Mother is busy in the kitchen and does not believe her. Annie runs to the hallway and dials the Police.

PC Bumble congratulates Annie

PC BUMBLE: Well done young lady. We always keep an eye out for 'odd sorts' & catching this zombie before it could do any more damage was just smashing!

ANNIE: It's all thanks to my Bumper Book of the Dead!

HOME PREPARATION AND DEFENCE

HOW TO SURVIVE A ZOMBIE SIEGE

The few first weeks of the zombie apocalypse will be open season for the walking dead. The unprepared will be stuck in their cars on blocked highways. Looters will be breaking into shops, oblivious to the risks around them. Hungry survivors with inadequate food supplies will soon be driven on to the streets foraging.

However, this 'time of plenty' will not last for the zombies and they will eventually turn their attention to the remaining survivors as they cower, fortified within their homes. Picture it: you wake up one day, look outside only to find a sea of dead eyes looking hungrily back at you. It could be hundreds. It could even be thousands. You are under zombie siege and you need to be prepared for the challenge.

There are four key interlinking strategies to surviving a zombie siege:

1 KEEPING DISCIPLINE
You must maintain order and control within the group to survive

2 STAYING STRONG
Personal fitness is important. Regularly check your defences

3 RESOURCE MANAGEMENT
Start tracking your supplies from day one of the siege

4 HAVE A PLAN B
Always prepare an escape plan or plans from any situation

SIEGE STRATEGIES

Providing you have the supplies, or can at least sneak out to top up essential items, most well-fortified sites will be able to last indefinitely against the dead. There is always a chance that the zombies will become distracted by easier meals elsewhere.

However, if the dead maintain their vigil and your supplies are down to a week or less then you should consider a breakout. This complex manoeuvre will involve some careful planning.

1 You should use any distraction techniques you can to divert the dead from your intended exit.

2 The whole group should be ready with their Bug-Out Bags and weapons.

3 Everyone should know the agreed Bug-Out location. You may choose to scatter in different directions, but be precise on where to meet up.

SURVIVING A ZOMBIE SIEGE

▶ Monitoring and reinforcing your fortifications must be your first priority. Remember to fortify in a systematic fashion so that if one layer is overrun, you simply fall back.

▶ Manage your resources from day one. Ration food and water. Maintain strict discipline on supplies and supplement with rainwater and food you've grown.

▶ Start planning an escape route. Useful options can be across roofs or through lofts into neighbouring houses.

▶ Enforce a Daily Work Schedule – you must keep the besieged busy for at least 4–5 hours per day. Activities can include strengthening defences or perimeter patrol.

▶ Keep young survivors occupied with a range of games and activities.

▶ Invest in some ear plugs – the relentless drone of the dead can have a detrimental effect on the besieged, particularly at night.

▶ Lessons from Churchill – you must maintain a 100% belief that you will all make it through. Never let your fellow survivors see you questioning this assumption.

▶ UNDER SIEGE

1. Reinforced fencing checked regularly with increasing pressure.
2. Fellow survivor working on an escape route just in case.
3. Distracting techniques being used.
4. A skilled slinger taking pot shots to help manage boredom.
5. Off-duty survivors playing a board game and relaxing.
6. Earplugs – survivors sleeping soundly
7. Guard duty – a clear rota system.
8. Schedule on the wall – tasks for at least 4–5 hours a day.
9. Food and supplies checked and regularly audited. Rations managed.
10. Bug-Out Bags ready to go.
11. Doors reinforced.
12. A survivor gardening to keep up morale and food stocks. Also catching pigeons.
13. A survivor on a radio listening in case help is within reach.
14. Possible break-out vehicle on standby.
15. All windows have been barred and have steel shutters to create an additional perimeter.

HOME PREPARATION AND DEFENCE

SURVIVAL LOCATIONS

Whether you are a well-prepared zombie survivalist, with a robust 90-day plan to get you through the zombie apocalypse or someone who plans to 'take it as it comes' when the dead arrive, you will need to consider the best locations to hold out in. For many, their own home or apartment will be the logical choice whereas the unprepared may find themselves caught in the office as the dead come a munching. Working with a group of seasoned zombie survival experts, the Ministry of Zombies has produced the following analysis of typical survivor locations. Each profile includes a brief overview, followed by a breakdown of the advantages and disadvantages in terms of zombie defence. Remember, this is general advice. The sites will vary greatly according to factors ranging from proximity to the epicentre of the zombie outbreak and population density to country and climate. Many of the home fortification guidelines outlined above will serve the survivor equally well for these sites.

OTHER KEY FACTORS

Another key factor to consider is access to your chosen survival location. If you live close to the wilderness or a National Park then an isolated survival location might be within scope for you and your family. After all, with the warnings from your monitoring system, you'll be able to pack up and leave before the stories of people being eaten even hit our television screens. However, if you are in a city centre then the chaos will spread quicker once the word gets out and you don't want to be caught in queues of jammed traffic, in a car packed with supplies. You may as well put a neon sign on the car saying 'Please come and loot my supplies'.

Think carefully about access to any long-term survival locations. Many zombie survivalists plan to spend the first few months of the crisis in their own fortified homes before moving out to their longer term site once the initial chaos has died down. Remember, for this to work you'll need multiple routes and a well-researched travel plan as you and your group of survivors will be moving through the zombie-infested territory. Review the options on the next few pages and make your own notes. Decide whether you need a long-term location – consider factors such as water supply, food sources and the overall sustainability of your primary location. Any travel will be dangerous, particularly if you have family or survivors with limited mobility.

▶ RESIDENTIAL SITE

POKING AROUND OTHER PEOPLE'S HOMES

The easiest option when looking for a site to escape the zombies, particularly if you are caught out in the open, will be residential sites, but will the residents still be there? And, will they be human? An apartment block could be a perfect survival location with multiple flats to loot for supplies.

ADVANTAGES

▶ These sites are most common and with thousands fleeing the chaos, there will be no shortage of empty homes for you to explore.

▶ You can select a good defensive location, with a decent perimeter wall and other key zombie defence features such as double-glazing and a strong front door.

▶ It's a chance to live in the neighbourhood you've always wanted to.

▶ If you seal the ground floor and entrance of an apartment block, you can work your way methodically through the flats, securing supplies as you go. You may also be able to link up with other survivors and work on a plan to defend the block as a community.

DISADVANTAGES

▶ The original occupants may not be overwhelmed to see you busting through their window and threatening to take their supplies.

▶ The original occupants may be more interested in feasting on your flesh. Be prepared for terrible odours if you break into a 'dead house'.

▶ Many homes will be poorly set up in terms of zombie defence – if it had been on the owner's list of priorities then they probably wouldn't have fled.

SUITABILITY 👍👍👍👍👍

▶ POLICE STATION

DIAL 999 OR 911 TO SURVIVE THE ZOMBIES?

With dozens of officers, many of them armed, a fortified location at the centre of any anti-zombie actions and a dedicated force of men and women ready to serve and protect – the humble city police station sounds like the ideal location to hold out against the dead.

ADVANTAGES

▶ Likely to be the focus on any fight back against the dead in the first days of a zombie crisis.

▶ A good stock of firearms, ammunition and riot gear.

▶ Typically these sites are well-fortified, with barred lower windows and secure cells.

▶ A disciplined group of trained officers will make up an ideal early survivor group.

▶ A police station is the ideal place to start fighting the dead. It is likely that a cadre of officers will already be planning to start.

DISADVANTAGES

▶ Most stations will be on the frontline of the fight so expect infected individuals to be 'brought in for questioning' in the confusion before the word 'zombie' is used.

▶ Stations may be abandoned as officers flee to protect their own families and will become key sites for gangs and other aggressive looters looking for guns and other booty.

▶ These sites don't stock much in the way of food. Survivors cannot live on doughnuts alone.

SUITABILITY 👍👍👍👍👍

▶ THE OFFICE

END OF THE WORLD AND YOU'RE AT WORK

Picture it. It's a typical day at work. You are battling through a mountain of emails, only to be told that the dead are now feasting on the living outside. There is too much chaos to attempt the commute home and you are only armed with a half-full stapler and a degree in Business Studies.

ADVANTAGES

▶ Strong main doors should be easy enough to fortify. Don't forget to blockade the fire exits.

▶ Some buildings have their own emergency generators.

▶ Most office buildings now have a plethora of security features including shatter proof glass and CCTV.

▶ An open office layout may encourage creative solutions to battling the dead. You will also have a good supply of flipcharts and stationary so you can 'brainstorm' your way out of trouble.

DISADVANTAGES

▶ Most offices are built as shells and use weak plasterboard partitions to create internal rooms. These walls will not hold back the hungry hordes.

▶ Panicking work colleagues may not be the ideal material for your survivor group.

▶ Food will be limited to the mouldy remnants in the office fridge. Where there is a canteen, there may be more supplies.

▶ Do you really want to be trapped at work when the end of the world finally comes?

SUITABILITY 👍👍👍👍👍

HOME PREPARATION AND DEFENCE

▶ SHOPPING MALL

THE CLASSIC ZOMBIE SURVIVAL LOCATION

The latest fashions, acres of shop space and more coffee shops than a small city, a modern shopping mall offers some enticing options to a zombie survivalist. It's a legendary location to defend, made famous in movies/training films such as *Dawn of the Dead*.

ADVANTAGES

▶ Clothing, supplies and even firearms will be plentiful with multiple food outlets providing useful sources of food.

▶ Most modern shopping centres are flooded with natural light which will be useful if the electricity shuts down. Many also have their own electricity-generating capacity.

▶ There may be green space for you to start growing your own food.

▶ There is always plenty of parking and this will only get better during a zombie apocalypse.

DISADVANTAGES

▶ It would take a small army to secure the literally hundreds of doors and fire escapes. Maybe they were all locked when you arrived but you can't take that chance.

▶ These locations typically attract thousands of visitors and employ hundreds of people on site. If they're still there as zombies, a shopping mall will be a dangerous place to clear.

▶ A shopping mall is the number one location on every looter and bandit's list. It is not a question of if you have to defend the site against human raiders, it's a question of when.

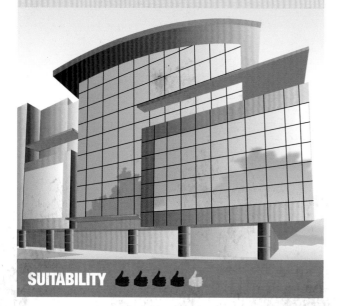

SUITABILITY 👍👍👍👍👍

▶ INDUSTRIAL SITE

A LONG SHIFT WILL MAKE THESE SITES SAFE

It's 0810hrs and you have just punched in 10 minutes late for your shift. But, good news. Your supervisor has been savaged by the dead on her way to work and half the staff are currently being mauled in the car park. Surviving the zombies in a factory or warehouse will present both challenges and opportunities.

ADVANTAGES

▶ Most sites will have a robust external security fence which can be sealed to create a secure perimeter.

▶ Any office areas are great locations to set up your 'home base' and canteen areas will provide good sources of supplies.

▶ Any roof tanks could provide a useful supply of water but always boil it before drinking.

▶ Many factories are well stocked with tools and other raw materials so there'll be no shortage of hand weapons such as hammers.

DISADVANTAGES

▶ A complex and confusing layout with multiple exits is not the easiest location to defend.

▶ The sheer size of these sites can make securing them a challenge.

▶ If horror movies have taught us anything, it is that most factories abound with hanging chains with a tendency to rust easily and move around in a spooky way, clinking as if something has just passed. No one wants that.

▶ These sites typically have large delivery doors which, if breached, could allow the dead to flood in.

SUITABILITY 👍👍👍👍👍

MINISTRY OF ZOMBIES

► PRISON

LOCKED UP MAY BE THE BEST PLACE TO BE

Well-fortified and secure, purpose-built modern prisons present some interesting opportunities and challenges to zombie survivalists. Ensure that you have scouted a prison before the zombies arrive if you intend to use it as a settlement location, preferably as a visitor rather than a permanent resident!

ADVANTAGES

▶ A robust external perimeter fence designed to keep people out as well as in. Add in guard towers and the ability to seal off areas and the modern prison complex is an easily defensible site.

▶ The location will include an armoury of weapons used by guards such as riot gear and firearms.

▶ Prisons have extensive catering, food and other facilities such as laundry etc. You will not be short of supplies in one of these locations.

DISADVANTAGES

▶ An interesting choice of either hundreds of dangerous criminals still locked in their cells after the guards have fled or legions of the infected hidden in endless corridors and dead ends.

▶ These sites will be first choice locations for any 'ex-cons' looking to start as a Robber Baron in the new world. Expect hordes of villains as well as the dead.

▶ Sprawling sites with hundreds of doors and locks may prove too much for smaller survivor groups.

SUITABILITY 👍👍👍👍👍

► BUNKER

SECRET BUNKER – WHAT COULD BE BETTER?

Whether you are buried deep in an underground shelter or defended by two-metre thick reinforced concrete, one thing is sure: neither zombies nor looters will be able to break into a sealed bunker easily. Once inside, you'll be safe and trapped in with the other survivors, or even alone. Remember to take a book.

ADVANTAGES

▶ They don't come much more secure than this. Once you seal that steel blast door, you are safe from virtually all attackers. Safe and sound, trapped in your bunker. That's good isn't it?

▶ A well-stocked bunker will be capable of supplying you with food, water and energy for years to come. You could hide there and wait for the whole thing to blow over.

▶ With a hidden entrance, no one is going to find you.

DISADVANTAGES

▶ Studies have shown that humans struggle with being 'trapped' underground for long periods of time. The lack of natural sunlight, fresh air and the development of 'cabin fever' are all potential risks.

▶ If you are sealed in a bunker or any location with the wrong people, it could be like being stuck in a never-ending episode of the *Kardashians* – with insanity and madness slowly developing.

▶ Simply hiding from the zombies won't make them go away. You could emerge after a year only to find millions of zombies in a land of the dead waiting to feast on you.

SUITABILITY 👍👍👍👍👍

HOME PREPARATION AND DEFENCE

▶ BOAT

A LIFE ON THE WAVES AWAY FROM DANGER

The option of living aboard a boat during a zombie outbreak has its attractions as you'd be away from the clawing hands of the dead and the violence and chaos as society crumbles. Zombies cannot swim but they do drift and bodies can float so you'll be safer apart from the risk of a ghoul clambering aboard.

ADVANTAGES

▶ Zombies have trouble with water. Apart from the danger of the odd floating dead, you'll be safe from the hordes off shore.
▶ Using a dinghy, you can make foraging trips ashore for supplies.
▶ Choose the right vessel and you could be set up for months. For example, a commercial whaler will cost around £300,000, has room for 15–20 survivors and can cover over 20,000 nautical miles on a single tank of fuel.

DISADVANTAGES

▶ At some point, you will need a land base for repairs, refuelling and supplies. Any serious damage to the boat could leave you and your survivor group in serious trouble.
▶ Many zombie survivalists favouring an escape by boat carefully make their plans and stock their craft only to ignore the fact that they will need to reach the vessels when the dead rise. Moreover, the chances are that the first panicky survivor who spots it in the marina will try to make off with it.
▶ It is estimated that piracy will increase exponentially during any zombie crisis.

SUITABILITY 👍👍👍👍👍

▶ MILITARY BASE

FIREPOWER TO DEFEAT THE WALKING DEAD?

Under the right leadership, military bases will become powerful bastions of humanity as the living battle the hordes of the dead. Could joining the army as they fight to survive be the best move, particularly if you live close to one of their bases? Bases could also become the focus of any human resistance against the zombies.

ADVANTAGES

▶ Well-armed and trained soldiers. Stockpiles of weapons and ammunition. The mouth-watering prospect of tanks and other armoured vehicles – with this kind of power, you can really take the war to the zombies.
▶ Most military sites have substantial stocks of tasteless c-rations or tinned 'combat meals'.
▶ These locations tend to be fortified with steel fences as an exterior barrier together with watch towers and controlled access points.

DISADVANTAGES

▶ Thousands of desperate civilians will make for these sites. Expect long queues as people are checked and massive traffic jams as the unprepared flock for the protection of the military.
▶ Some zombie survival experts predict that the military will disintegrate as the dead overrun the country, leaving only dangerous armed groups guarding these locations.
▶ There is a high likelihood that some rogue General will declare 'martial law' as the crisis develops and the discipline may become worse than a North Korean Summer Camp.

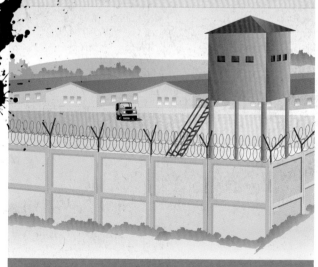

SUITABILITY 👍👍👍👍👍

▶ THE WILDERNESS

AWAY FROM THE HUSTLE AND BUSTLE

If you have access to a wilderness location, then getting away from urban concentrations will certainly help you dodge the hordes of dead that will be ravaging the streets. Key to this location will be access – have a good plan so that you get away before the rush to avoid that whole 'traffic jam bloodbath' scene.

ADVANTAGES

▶ Once well away from any main towns, cities or roads – you will be relatively safe from both zombies and any human attackers.
▶ Plenty of 'alone time' and the benefits of plenty of fresh air.
▶ You will have a chance to use all of that expensive camping and hiking gear you bought a few years ago.
▶ Growing a long beard can help you create a cool 'mountain man' look – providing you are male and have a chequered shirt.

DISADVANTAGES

▶ Surviving without hot showers may start to wear thin as winter sets in.
▶ Food can be scarce unless you have the hunting, fishing or foraging skills to provide for yourself and your group.
▶ You will need an excellent level of fitness and survival training to stay alive in winter or in hostile climates such as the jungle or desert.
▶ You will need to be able to cope with any medical emergency yourself or within the group. Fancy having a tooth out with only a handful of lingenberries as an anaesthetic?

SUITABILITY 👍👍👍👍👍

▶ DESERT ISLAND

A TROPICAL PARADISE FREE OF ZOMBIES

Cutting yourself off from the world can be appealing at the best of times. Add to that several million flesh-eating corpses and a tropical island starts to look like a very attractive proposition. You'll be away from those cold winters and you may even decide to build a house on the beach, complete with monkey waiters.

ADVANTAGES

▶ Complete zombie-free living in a tropical paradise location.
▶ Miles of golden sand and warm weather all year round, creating a holiday-like atmosphere for you and your survivor group.
▶ If you have a small boat, you can raid the mainland or nearby islands for those extra essentials.
▶ An endless supply of coconuts if it's a tropical island.

DISADVANTAGES

▶ An endless supply of coconuts and seafood. This is bad news if you don't like coconuts or seafood.
▶ There is a small risk that a stray corpse will wash up on your golden sands as you lay sunbathing.
▶ How in the world are you going to get there? Direct flights will be hard to come by after the zombie apocalypse.
▶ If you make it, being cut off from the world has its downsides. Your social life will certainly tail off.
▶ If you think your island is a paradise, so will others. Soon, your monkey waiters could be serving drinks to some cruel pirate as you are working in the fields to grow your new masters more food.

SUITABILITY 👍👍👍👍👍

THE PERFECT ZOMBIE-PROOF LOCATION

No Man's Land Fort was built in the 1860's off the coast of Portsmouth, England. Originally constructed to defend against French invaders, it has now been converted into a luxury hotel with more than 20 rooms, two helipads and a heated indoor swimming pool. The fort is about a mile from the mainland and rises over 60 feet above the sea. At today's prices, it would cost around £150m to build.

Whilst no one site could ever be said to be the perfect zombie-proof location, this fort comes close and with an additional expenditure of around £25m, it could be transformed into the zombie-proof fortress below. Remember, you may be able to source a similar primary site wherever you are in the world and several zombie-fighting groups are looking at 'crowd funding' their own perfect zombie hideouts. You will need a good sized site with obvious zombie-proofing potential, but it need not be a purpose-designed fortification. It could be an old factory with a particularly strong exterior fence, or an isolated hotel with plenty of space for growing your own crops. What is shown here is simply an example of what can be achieved.

CROWD FUNDING A ZOMBIE FORTRESS

Investing in the creation of an ideal anti-zombie fortress will doubtless cost millions. It doesn't matter if you buy some isolated plot of land in the Australian outback or convert a historic sea fort – you will require substantial financial resources to complete a grand plan like this. Many sites will come as a shell in terms of zombie defence, meaning that you will need to add on the costs of improving the site as well as the initial purchase.

However, it is possible to join forces with other zombie survivalists and 'crowd fund' a defensive site. This means developing a group of friends or family who commit resources to a central fund and this is then used to create your zombie outbreak hideaway. You can find out more about these funds on many of the zombie survival forums on the internet. One group of survivalists in Glasgow has already purchased an island off the West Coast of Scotland and is currently constructing a village of ten homes with a surrounding steel fence. The group also has a boat in Glasgow which they plan to use as part of their Bug-Out plan. It will shuttle to and from the port taking survivors to their long-term settlement location. At least that's the theory!

DEVELOPING A 'SURVIVAL NARRATIVE'

A survey by *Survivor Magazine* revealed that whilst 78% of respondents who had a prepared long-term location felt they have detailed plans on how to reach their secure basis in crisis, less than 23% had any real plan on what they were going to do as the weeks of isolation dragged on. Few were able to answer the underlying question – 'what's the long-term plan once you reach your fortress?' Family members and fellow survivors will start to ask what the plan is and how long you can last. You may not have all the answers but you need to have a 'survival narrative' which provides them with some level of response and you need to be consistent in this area.

▶ 'ONCE WE ARE IN OUR SECURE FORTRESS, WE WILL RUN SILENT FOR THE FIRST MONTH OF THE CRISIS. THIS TIME WILL BE ABOUT STOCK TAKING, SECURING OUR POSITION AND SEEING OUT THE INITIAL CHAOS OF THE OUTBREAK.'
Be firm here, don't be pressured into moving too fast – there will be countless rumours of safe zones and many of these will be just rumours. Ensure that the group understands the danger of being 'out on the road'.

▶ 'AFTER THIS PERIOD, WE WILL REVIEW THE SITUATION AND CONSIDER SENDING OUT FACT-FINDING PATROLS OR SCOUTS IF IT'S SAFE TO DO SO. YOU MAY BE ABLE TO MONITOR EMERGENCY BROADCASTS AND GET THIS INFORMATION.'
Be sure that you do not alert other desperate survivors to your safe location unless you have the resources to take more people in.

▶ 'OUR LONG-TERM PLAN IS TO STAY SECURE IN THE BUNKER FOR AT LEAST 90 DAYS AND TO REVIEW LONGER TERM OPTIONS DURING THIS PERIOD. IF WE CAN EXPAND OUR CURRENT LOCATION THEN WE MAY USE IT AS A LONG-TERM SETTLEMENT LOCATION. IF NOT, WE WILL CONSIDER ONE OF THE ALPHA SITES ALREADY IDENTIFIED.'
Again, be clear and decisive on this. Fellow survivors will raise all sorts of crazy ideas which will almost certainly involve your group heading off in bandit country on a fool's errand.

Build your survival narrative around these kinds of statements. Survivors will be scared enough as it is so any degree of security you can provide will be welcome. Remember, you may not have all the answers, you may not even believe 100% in what you're saying but as a leader you will need to stay strong and adapt as required.

▶ NO MAN'S LAND FORT

1. Mounted M60s placed strategically around the fort to defend against pirates.
2. Over sixty feet above sea level so no zombie can clamber up and so protect the fort from rough seas.
3. A secured launch for raiding the mainland for supplies and searching for survivors.
4. A helicopter and helipad, perfect for longer range air patrols. Kit also includes several heli-drones which can be flown over the mainland.
5. Extensive roof gardens and greenhouses for fresh fruit and vegetables, protected from sea-spray by toughened glass
6. 10 foot thick concrete walls, able to resist all small arms fire and many other guns and missiles.

7. A fully-equipped hydroelectric generator deep within the fort.
8. Aviation fuel for the helicopter and a full stock of spare parts.
9. Command tower which can also be sealed if the fort is over-run, allowing secure access to the helipad.
10. A fully equipped armoury and workshop.
11. Living quarters for up to 100 within the fort, including a canteen and medical bay.
12. A radar guided anti-missile gun – controlled from the command post.
13. A defensive array of surface to surface missiles to target hostile vessels or locations on the mainland.

14. A secure walkway for armed foot patrols and lookouts.
15. An expansive reinforced glass dome to maximise natural light within the fort interior.
16. Fort is built using a rocky outcrop as a foundation, over two miles from the coast.
17. A fresh water bore hole has been sunk into the rock below the fort and now provides the sea-fort with drinking water.
18. A satellite and listening dish monitors world events as well as getting updates from any satellites still operational.
19. A glass conservatory with a library and comfortable chairs for relaxing.
20. A fully equipped communications centre which also doubles as a cinema complex for survivors.

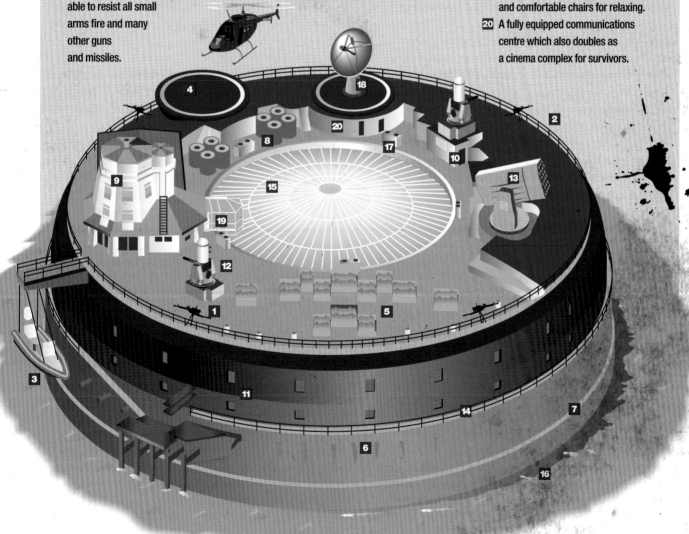

ZOMBIE COMBAT AND WEAPONS

So far we've learnt what zombies are, the risks they pose to the living and how they can be killed or at least the theory of how to kill them. But now it's time to face up to some unpleasant facts.

Firstly, when the zombies take over humanity will no longer be top of the food chain. We will no longer be able to wander the streets confident that, unless savaged by an escaped tiger, we can safely handle any wildlife around. Sure, some folks will live in the wilds and will be wary of bears or snakes, but for most, an angry squirrel or moody rabbit holds no fear. This will all change after the zombie apocalypse.

Secondly, whilst you may have already realised that a single zombie can be clumsy, slow and not particularly well furnished in the brain department, it is nonetheless a potentially deadly opponent. Add to this that zombies frequently cluster and will often attack in 'hordes' then you soon realise the importance of understanding how to fight these creatures. They aren't going to leave you alone. There won't be any uneasy truce. They will come at you, your family and any survivors for as long as they are able.

This is why zombie combat should be central to any survival preparation, as sooner or later you will find yourself facing the walking dead.

ZOMBIE COMBAT

Every fighter has their own favourite technique or specialised weapon but the advice for beginners is to work your way methodically through the next few pages. Learn about **S.T.E.N.C.H.**, absorb the information about your enemy and practise both the unarmed and armed combat moves. Hopefully, you'll never face the dead without a weapon, but be prepared just in case and you'll have a better chance of staying alive. You should schedule zombie combat practice sessions for at least an hour a day.

Finally, remember to adapt these plans and tips to your own needs or those in your group. These are general guidelines, but you can always 'spice' them up with your own homemade weapons or adapt them so that others can defend themselves.

EVERYONE IN YOUR GROUP MUST BE ABLE TO FIGHT TO SOME DEGREE SO YOU COULD WELL END UP BECOMING A ZOMBIE COMBAT TRAINER BUT FOR NOW, READ ON AND TAKE NOTES

ZOMBIE COMBAT AND WEAPONS
YOUR LAST ZOMBIE KILL

Before considering combat and weapons any further, it is important to be clear that the majority of zombies killed by human survivors are killed by clubbing weapons. In a recent Ministry of Zombies survey more than 43% of zombie kills were made using a club-like weapon. We strongly advise that you always carry a clubbing weapon as a reserve to your main weapon.

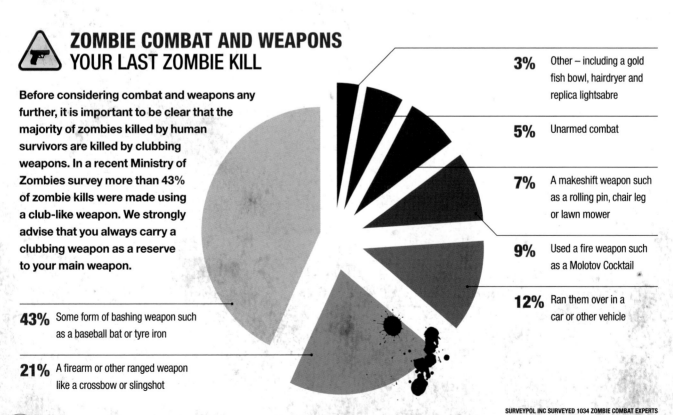

3% Other – including a gold fish bowl, hairdryer and replica lightsabre

5% Unarmed combat

7% A makeshift weapon such as a rolling pin, chair leg or lawn mower

9% Used a fire weapon such as a Molotov Cocktail

12% Ran them over in a car or other vehicle

43% Some form of bashing weapon such as a baseball bat or tyre iron

21% A firearm or other ranged weapon like a crossbow or slingshot

SURVEYPOL INC SURVEYED 1034 ZOMBIE COMBAT EXPERTS

MINISTRY OF ZOMBIES

THE WEAPONS OF A ZOMBIE
S.T.E.N.C.H.

SALIVA	Infected fluid – saliva and blood
TEETH	Sharp, jagged incisors
ENERGY	Consistent level of power
NAILS	Jagged weapons, like claws
CEASELESS	Won't stop, won't be scared off
HUNGER	Driven 100% by this hunger

Infected **SALIVA** dripping from the mouth. Where this is dry, it may be replaced by putrid bile or pus, which is just as deadly.

The dead have poor dental hygiene. **TEETH** tend to yellow under the zombic condition and endless gnawing on human bones frequently creates sharp and jagged incisors. Some zombiologists see this as nature's way of arming the carnivore!

The dead have seemingly boundless **ENERGY**. There are chemical and biological processes at work enabling zombie muscle mass to 'feed' on any fat within the corpse.

Whilst the finger **NAILS** do tend to grow after death, it is a slight retraction in the skin around the nail which gives it that dagger-like appearance. Again, endless scratching and foraging create sharp weapons riddled with infection and bacteria. With time, however, the nails may fall off.

A zombie is **CEASELESS** in its quest for human flesh. Zombie psychologists suggest that the dead see the living as having a warm golden glow around them. They are therefore obsessed with ingesting this 'lost life force'.

This **HUNGER** can never be abated. A zombie will cram living flesh into its mouth until its stomach cavity is at bursting point. How the dead break down food into energy is not yet fully understood. Few have the constitution to open up a zombie gut and review what's inside.

NOW CLOSE THIS BOOK AND TEST YOUR KNOWLEDGE: NAME THE KEY WEAPONS OF A ZOMBIE USING S.T.E.N.C.H.

ZOMBIE COMBAT AND WEAPONS

UNARMED COMBAT AGAINST THE DEAD

Make no mistake about it, no unarmed combat against the walking dead will ever be safe. Close combat with the infected is a dangerous business in which the living may be bitten or scratched at any time, not to mention the obvious health issues of tangling with a rotting corpse. It is advised that survivors carry at least a hand weapon at all times, be this a small hammer or even a large dagger.

However, there may be times when you do come face to face with the zombies and are unarmed. The following guidelines are designed for these occasions. Hopefully, you will never have to use them in combat, but ensure you know and practise the basic manoeuvres. It could

mean the difference between you living to fight another day or becoming a buffet snack for a horde of the dead. Remember that unarmed combat must be supported by a comprehensive physical fitness training programme. It's no use going for that lunge only to find that you pull a muscle or that you lack the strength to really drive a fist into that rotting zombie brain. The moves outlined over the next few pages do not demand any specific combat training, but they do require practice and that you achieve a reasonable level of fitness. You should consult a medical professional before starting any form of zombie unarmed combat training.

▶ DEFENSIVE MOVES

There are four classic defensive moves a fighter can use to defend a zombie attack: blocking, the neck grab, double-handed shove and the standard punch. There are hundreds of variants of these main types, but on the whole these four will be a powerful arsenal for those just looking to make a break for it at the first opportunity.

Ensure that you understand the three core principles before you start to practise these moves: your body must be in balance, your mind focused on the job in hand and remember that your objective is to create the room to escape – not to look like Bruce Lee in front of other survivors.

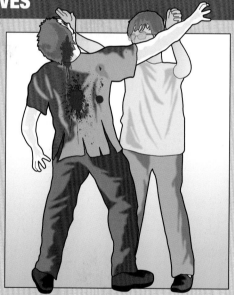

DEFENSIVE MOVE 1
BLOCKING
Remember a zombie has two primary vectors of attack – the grabbing claws and the snapping jaws. In close combat with the dead, you must always target these two areas as illustrated by our combatant in this figure. Here we are blocking both the oncoming jaw and the clubbing arm.

DEFENSIVE MOVE 2
NECK GRAB OR 'PIN'
Disabling a zombie's main weapon is a useful strategy if you are defending in confined spaces. Pin the ghoul by the throat, leveraging its jaw upwards and away from your holding arm. Squeezing the corpse's throat will do no damage and may lead to the head collapsing forward. Also, always uses your spare hand to deal the 'death blow'. Remember, the zombie will still have its arms.

THE CORE PRINCIPLES
Written down over 1,000 years ago, they still form the foundation of all self-defence against the dead.

THE BODY IS BALANCE
You should be fit, steady and standing on both feet.

THE MIND IS STEADY
Your mind must not succumb to panic. Your mind should be clear and braced for combat.

CREATE THE ROOM TO ESCAPE
Remember that the objective is to disable the dead to create space for your escape.

> ONLY THE SUICIDAL WOULD ENGAGE THE DEAD IN PROLONGED HAND-TO-HAND COMBAT. IT IS LIKE A MAN FIGHTING AGAINST THE TIDE. SOON, HE WILL BE OVERCOME BY EITHER THEIR TEETH OR THEIR BLOOD.

TZU SAN LEE,
JOURNAL OF A YUNNAN PROVINCE ADMINISTRATION, 1220

In modern terms, you must be combat-ready at all times. You must be fit and agile, with your mind fully focused. Remain cool and calm in action – if you are to survive, you need to move like a warrior. If you find yourself without a weapon, have a good look around you – most locations will yield at least some items you can use as hand-held weapons.

DEFENSIVE MOVE 3
DOUBLE-HANDED SHOVE
This is a simple but effective move to give you that extra room to make your escape. It involves the fighter taking a firm footing, then pushing both arms forward towards the zombie, with hands out flat to meet the creature. The target area should be the upper chest and the force should cause the zombie to fall backwards or at least be pushed away. Do not attempt this move on any zombie that appears to be in an advanced stage of decay or with an obvious chest wound or you could end up with your hands buried, or worse, stuck in the chest cavity of the ghoul.

DEFENSIVE MOVE 4
STANDARD PUNCH
Unless you are wearing strong protective gloves, a punch to a zombie should always be delivered to the side of the jaw or, if the target is unclear, the side of the head. A direct punch to the front increases the risk of your fist being punctured by the ghoul's sharp, jagged and infected teeth. A powerful swinging punch from the side can take the lower jaw off, rendering the zombie unable to bite down. Never punch a zombie in the mid-section – the creature will not be wounded and it is likely to bury its face in your body.

ZOMBIE COMBAT AND WEAPONS

THE DIFFERENCE IN FIGHTING THE DEAD

There are some important differences when facing a zombie in unarmed combat and those experienced in martial arts or self-defence sometimes struggle to fully grasp this rule change. To be clear, traditional combat techniques used against the living need to be adapted for use against the walking dead. In general, the martial arts and any intensive fitness training will provide a good foundation for unarmed combat against zombies, but it is often the case that experienced martial artists do not appreciate the great difference between battling a living opponent in a training dojo and taking on several ravenous zombies on a street corner.

▶ Vulnerable points on a human, such as solar plexus, groin or bridge of the nose are not appropriate to zombies who have no feeling in these areas.

▶ A classic low karate kick may work to disable a living opponent but against zombies it will send the ghoul forward, its jagged nails outstretched. The most likely outcome is a 'raking' by which the dead drag their infected nails down you as they fall.

▶ The dead obey no rules other than the one that makes them want to feast on your flesh. Some martial artists come from such a disciplined background that they forget a zombie has no honour and feels no mercy or pain.

▶ BASIC UNARMED COMBAT MOVES

There will be occasions when blocking is simply not enough. You may need to seriously impair or damage your attacker. There are four basic moves in a typical zombie self-defence programme: the Queensberry blast, the upper cut, the 'Captain Kirk' and the low knee kick and dash.

Three of these moves are made using the arms as they are traditionally the easiest for beginners to master without losing their balance and are most instinctive. We start with a variation of the standard punch which is a core move in any unarmed combat defence programme.

BASIC MOVE 1
QUEENSBERRY BLAST

The fighter must adopt a classic boxer stance, with one leg slightly forward. The Queensberry Blast is a natural combination of two jabs to the upper half of the zombie head. The punches should land in rapid succession and it is likely that the force will lead the corpse to stumble backwards. It is a low-energy move that can be useful where the fighter lacks the strength to take out the zombie with one punch.

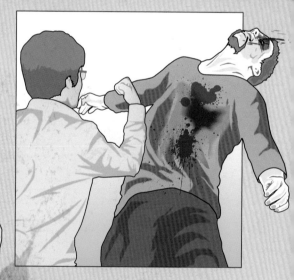

BASIC MOVE 2
UPPER CUT

Similar to a standard punch, this upward sweeping blow can prove fatal to a zombie when delivered with enough force. The user shifts onto one side, swings an arm back and delivers the punch directly underneath the chin, forcing the corpse's head to whip back. It can be a powerful punch to disable a zombie with, but sometimes it leaves the dead with a shattered row of sharp teeth – something they will be thankful for as it makes it easier to pierce through living flesh.

- However, a kick to the knee or gouging of the eyes can still 'damage' a zombie's movement or sight. Just be aware that pain and any disability will have no impact on the dead's desire to feed on the living. If these walking corpses get the chance, they will munch down hard on your flesh.
- Classic self-defence and martial arts holds rely on leveraging an opponent and using pain to restrict their movements. Few of these techniques will work on the dead.

IF YOU HAVE BEEN TRAINED IN ANY COMBAT TECHNIQUES, THE BEST ADVICE IS TO FORGET WHAT YOU HAVE LEARNT. MANY TRADITIONAL MOVES WILL BE SUICIDAL AGAINST THE DEAD.

BASIC MOVE 3
THE 'CAPTAIN KIRK'

Supposedly taught to William Shatner by an ex-Army Ranger stuntman, his trademark double-handed punch is particularly effective against the dead when delivered from behind. With force and making contact with the mid-back section, it will drive the zombie face down to the ground, making for an easy stamping target. Delivering a double-handed punch to the front is similar but involves whipping the hands out of harm's way much quicker. Shatner himself always preferred two punches, one to the middle then a knock down to the back of your opponent.

BASIC MOVE 4
LOW KNEE KICK & DASH

The most useful move in combat against the undead is the low knee kick, which will temporarily disable the zombie and enable you to make your escape. The move is most effectively delivered when the kick strikes the side of the knee, almost in a stamping motion. Be especially wary of the corpse's direction of fall and remember that this will not disable the ghoul's snapping jaws. This move will leave an active crawler behind even if you manage to shatter the knee joint. Remember, this is not a kill move – it's a basic move designed to give you time to make a run for it.

ZOMBIE COMBAT AND WEAPONS

NO HEROICS

Where you can make a run for it, do so – there is nothing heroic about hand-to-hand combat with the dead. But if you're going to stand your ground, never attempt to face the undead in unarmed combat if there is a weapon to hand. Grab what you can and use it! Here are a few examples you may not have considered.

ON UNDERGROUND GOING TO WORK?

Use the train doors to crush the zombie's head. If they are already in the carriage, grab a shopping bag and swing it round Wild West style. Kick the zombie off the platform towards an oncoming train. Of course, this would delay your trip.

QUEUING AT THE SUPERMARKET?

Throw expensive spirits on the zombies and then skilfully flick a match. Saving that, a frozen turkey to the head is a powerful clubbing weapon. If you are a sports fan and have the skills, you may be able to take a zombie down by throwing a can and hitting the ghoul in the head.

IN CHURCH?

Throwing piles of dusty hymn books will knock the dead over from a distance. Try to use the ones with musical guidelines as they tend to be thicker. If your priest is Irish, he may be quite handy himself and will be able to support you in any combat.

▶ ADVANCED UNARMED COMBAT MOVES

Once a fighter has mastered the basic moves in combat, there are hundreds of more advanced techniques that can be learnt. Some will take months of practice, but many offer breathtaking alternatives to use in action, with moves that can save lives and take out multiple zombies at a time. Start your training by learning basic kick moves. A simple kick to the chest will often send a zombie tumbling to the ground, but ensure that you have the balance to stay on your feet before trying to kick any higher – remember the core principles of combat against the undead – balance, clear mind and room to escape.

ADVANCED MOVE 1
HIGH HEAD KICK

Much maligned in normal self-defence for leaving its proponent vulnerable to counter attack, against the undead a well-placed kick can knock a zombie down, and in the cases of extremely desiccated creatures take their heads off completely. The user must be fit and limber to use this move. Pulling a muscle in unarmed combat against the dead will reduce the principal advantage you have over the zombies, which is your speed.

ADVANCED MOVE 2
THE 360 TORNADO KICK

This move is specifically designed to knock down multiple undead opponents. The fighter swings their legs back before jumping high into the air to deliver their first blow. Using the momentum of the swing, the leg should then follow round, hitting one target after another in a circular motion. All of the momentum will be driven into your lead or landing leg to deliver the multiple blows. It can appear as if the fighter is 'floating' so this is one impressive move.

ZOMBIE COMBAT AND WEAPONS
THE SOUTHERN PRAYING MANTIS

This is a complete system of combat specifically designed for use against zombies. Thought to originate in the monasteries of the Wudang Mountains in China, this highly skilled art has an emphasis on rapid hand work and short kicks, many of them low. Little is known of this art in the West and it has tantalised martial fanatics around the world to hear of the moves such as Sarm Bo Jin, which literally means 'Three Step Arrow'. The few accounts we have compare the style to that of a graceful street fighter. If you can obtain training in this art then this is the perfect preparation for the zombie apocalypse. According to Chinese zombie experts, an elderly monk known only as Zhang Sanfung is the only living master of the Southern Praying Mantis.

REMEMBER THE CORE PRINCIPLES OF COMBAT AGAINST THE UNDEAD – BALANCE, CLEAR MIND AND ROOM TO ESCAPE

ADVANCED MOVE 3
DOUBLE DROP KICK

This is an advanced move that requires great agility, but it can deliver a powerful, even knockout, blow to a zombie. Users require a good run up followed by a flying leap towards the undead opponent. The two feet should land squarely on the chest and the force will send the ghoul tumbling backwards. A disadvantage of this technique is that the user is left prone and vulnerable on the floor for a few seconds. However, it can be most useful if a zombie is threatening multiple targets and you just need to get the creature well away, for example from children or wounded.

ADVANCED MOVE 4
THE AERIAL

This is basically a forward somersault, normally with hands. The kicking leg swings over the top and lands with incredible force on the top of the zombie. The trick is to kick up your back leg as you take off. As your body gains velocity, the leg flips forward causing the body to flip and the foot to come down with skull-crushing force. This is really a show move and any slip-ups will leave you prone to counterattack by your ghoulish opponent. However, pull it off and you will appear to any watching survivors to be the post-apocalyptic equivalent of Bruce Lee.

ZOMBIE COMBAT AND WEAPONS

ARMED COMBAT AGAINST ZOMBIES

Within weeks of a major zombie outbreak, the walking dead will outnumber the living by thousands to one. Survivors will no doubt become experts with their trusty hand weapons, but they will need some serious firepower if they are to even up the odds.

Studies have shown that survivors do not need access to firearms to survive the walking dead. Preparation, training and a survivor mentality can be enough to get you through. So, guns are not an essential aspect of preparation for the zombie apocalypse, and in any case in most parts of the world their ownership and use is heavily regulated. However, someone 'tooled' up and trained will be in a stronger position to fend off the dead.

 IMPORTANT

ALWAYS REMEMBER THAT THE OWNERSHIP AND USE OF FIREARMS IS CONTROLLED BY LEGISLATION. ZOMBIE SURVIVAL IS ABOUT KEEPING YOURSELF AND YOUR FELLOW SURVIVORS ALIVE, NOT CREATING HASSLE FOR THE POLICE. ALL ZOMBIE SURVIVALISTS MUST ENSURE THAT THEY ADHERE TO ALL LEGAL REQUIREMENTS AND ARE FULLY TRAINED TO USE THE WEAPONS DESCRIBED IN THIS MANUAL. BE LEGAL. BE SAFE. BE TRAINED. AND, PLAY NICELY OUT THERE, KIDDIES.

A PRIMER ON ZOMBIE KILLING WITH GUNS

HANDGUN

RANGE: **SHORT**
WEIGHT: **LIGHT**

Close-range head shots below 10 metres. Ideally, every fighter should be equipped with a handgun. They can be secured safely around the belt.

RIFLE/ASSAULT RIFLE

RANGE: **MEDIUM**
WEIGHT: **MEDIUM**

Perfect for sweeping small hordes of the dead and mobile firing. Every patrol or foraging team should be equipped with at least one rifle.

SHOTGUN

RANGE: **SHORT**
WEIGHT: **MEDIUM**

Ideal for in-building combat or bursts into tightly packed hordes. It is good practice to have a 'shotgun fighter' covering your foraging group when inside buildings.

MACHINE GUN

RANGE: **MEDIUM–LONG**
WEIGHT: **HEAVY**

Perfect for sweeping advancing hordes and defending survivor settlements from a fixed firing position.

REMEMBER: A ZOMBIE SURVIVALIST USES THE RIGHT GUN FOR THE RIGHT JOB AND A HEAD SHOT WILL PUT A ZOMBIE DOWN FOR GOOD

DON'T SHOOT YOURSELF

Even if this doesn't kill you, you'll be slowed down and the scent of blood will attract hordes of the dead.

NEVER, EVER POINT GUNS AT HUMANS

Loaded or not, never point a gun at another human being unless you are in combat. For the untrained idiot, there's more chance that you'll shoot a fellow survivor as you do your Robert De Niro impressions.

NEVER FIRE OFF ALL OF YOUR AMMUNITION

A full clip can make the gun amateur feel very powerful but on fully automatic it can empty in just a few seconds. Don't forget to maintain your weapon. No matter which gun you use, all require care and maintenance. Imagine yourself trying to reload your Grandad's antique flintlock musket with the ghouls bearing down on you.

DON'T BE A POOR SHOT

It is no exaggeration to say that only an accomplished marksman will be able to get the kind of head shots needed to take down a zombie. Others may be able to hit limbs and slow down the dead, but more often than not inaccurate shooting under very stressful conditions will put them on the menu.

DON'T BECOME OVER-CONFIDENT

Firearms have that effect on people. Just remember, no matter how many handguns or rifles you have, the dead only need a small chance to bite or scratch you and it's game over, man. To paraphrase Darth Vader, do not over-estimate the power of the technology you have created.

 MINISTRY OF ZOMBIES

HANDGUNS

More common than larger firearms, many police and security forces around the world are armed with side arms. They are generally light with little recoil and are ideal for close combat against the dead. The Beretta 92F is an ideal balance of firepower, reliability and weight, making it the favoured handgun choice of many zombie survivalists. However, there are hundreds of different guns out there so review your options carefully and remember that in terms of maintenance, spare parts and ammunition, it is easier if your group is equipped with the same or similar models.

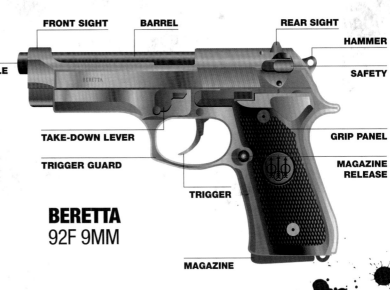

FRONT SIGHT · **BARREL** · **REAR SIGHT** · **HAMMER** · **MUZZLE** · **SAFETY** · **TAKE-DOWN LEVER** · **GRIP PANEL** · **TRIGGER GUARD** · **MAGAZINE RELEASE** · **TRIGGER** · **MAGAZINE**

BERETTA
92F 9MM

EXPERIENCE COUNTS

In a Ministry of Zombies field study at three gun clubs in the USA, only 30% of experienced shooters achieve a 'kill shot' on zombies at 30 metres. To those trained in the use of firearms, the kill figures below may look lower than one might expect from a group of experienced shooters. However, during this live-fire exercise, combat conditions were simulated to disrupt and distract. For example, loud klaxons were played and targets moved, simulating a real zombie. This field study confirmed that even the most experienced shooters struggled to make a kill shot with a handgun at over 20 metres. The lesson is therefore that a pistol is a close-range weapon of last resort except for a very skilful shooter with cast-iron nerves.

RANGE	% 'KILL SHOT'
50 metres	10%
40 metres	13%
30 metres	30%
20 metres	45%
Below 10 metres	71%

This field study was completed in April 2012, involving 167 shooters, all with at least two years' experience.

HANDGUN INSTRUCTIONS

1 Always read the product manual. A firearm is not a DVD player and you do need to know how to use all of its functionality against zombies.

2 Keep it locked and unloaded when not out and about in zombietown.

3 Learn how to reload properly and how to complete the exercise under time pressure. Getting a magazine jammed with any firearm could get you killed.

4 When in combat, draw your weapon and ensure that the safety is off. Hold the gun steadily and be aware of nervous trembling, which could disrupt your shot.

5 Identify your target. Know the signs of a zombie. A warning may be used if appropriate.

6 Your stance should be your strongest foot in front with your pelvis turned 45 degrees towards the attacking zombie.

7 Breathe slowly and aim at the face of the zombie. Most panicking fighters tend to shoot high so a good strategy is to aim for the lower neck or torso. Pull the trigger in a smooth motion.

8 If your target has been dispatched, move on. If not, complete a stamp to the head with your boot to destroy the zombie. Be aware that the loud crack of a pistol or any firearm will attract more of the dead, so each time you use your gun, balance carefully the options you have. Could you, for example, take out the zombie with a clubbing weapon instead?

CLOSE-RANGE HANDGUN SHOT

If they have the weapons, every survivor should be armed and trained with a handgun for emergency self-defence. It may be used when noise is not an issue or a fighter just needs to 'get the job done'. The ideal distance for the average shooter is less than 10 metres – any more and accuracy will suffer. The fighter must pause for a few seconds and regulate their breathing before smoothly squeezing off one round. A full-face shot from this distance will take out a zombie in more than 87% of cases, depending on the gun.

ZOMBIE COMBAT AND WEAPONS

RIFLES AND ASSAULT RIFLES

In the hands of a skilled marksman, both bolt-action and semi-automatic rifles have excellent accuracy and can kill at considerable distance. They are also a major deterrent to any human raiders who wander your way. However, the same rules apply in terms of accuracy. It will require a head shot to take the zombie down permanently although the power of some of these weapons means that even glancing head shots can often reach the magic '80% of brain destroyed' mark.

TAKING DOWN THE DEAD WITH RIFLES

Where you are directing a team of low-skilled and panicky fire teams there are two important things you should do. Firstly, ensure that all weapons are on single shot and be firm when having the fire teams hold fire. Secondly, constantly remind the teams to shoot low – aiming for the legs. This will ensure that every shot counts no matter how inaccurate.

Zombie combat experts have endlessly debated the value of a non-kill shot to a zombie. For example, whilst some argue that at least it takes them out of the game, others insist you are merely creating a different kind of monster, a crawler, which may still cause you issues. It is good practice to have a few in your group armed with just melee weapons to be sure that any zombies close by can be taken care of. Also, there may be times when a silent kill is required. Even if you are out of ammunition, it may still be worth having one of the team carry a rifle as it can act as a deterrent to thieves and looters.

THE TYPE 51 AK-47Z ASSAULT RIFLE

This is the world's first purpose-built anti-zombie assault rifle. Currently only in use in China and North Korea, it shares the best features of the AK range, being easy to fire, maintain and strip down. It is also one of the most durable and robust assault rifles in the world. However, the 'Z' version of the weapon cannot be fired on fully automatic and has been adapted to fire special plastic dum-dum bullets, which come in either a standard 40-round magazine or a mouth-watering 120-round drum. These projectiles are fired at a much lower velocity than the standard AK-47 and the plastic bullets have a flat end designed to make maximum impact on the brittle skull and mashed brain of a zombie. According to the Red Army, head shots from high-velocity modern weapons are likely to pass directly through a zombie brain without doing sufficient destruction to take out the ghoul. The AK-47Z on the other hand is a purpose designed zombie killer.

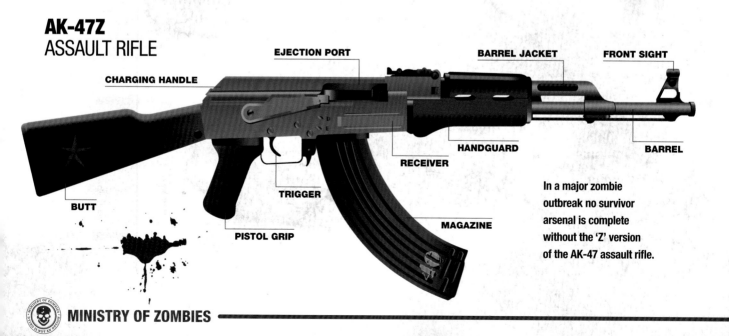

AK-47Z
ASSAULT RIFLE

EJECTION PORT

CHARGING HANDLE

BARREL JACKET

FRONT SIGHT

HANDGUARD

BARREL

RECEIVER

TRIGGER

BUTT

PISTOL GRIP

MAGAZINE

In a major zombie outbreak no survivor arsenal is complete without the 'Z' version of the AK-47 assault rifle.

PROCURING AN AK-47Z ASSAULT RIFLE

For anyone who is legally permitted to own such a weapon, the Chinese government has recently introduced a scheme to help zombie survivors procure an AK-47Z at very reasonable cost. However, the process is very bureaucratic and an application must be made to the Red Army offices in Beijing for permission before applying again to your local Chinese Embassy. You are required to pass three tests for approval:

1 You must include documented proof that you can legally hold a firearm in your country.

2 You must demonstrate that you hold socialist values or at least an appreciation of the revolution.

3 You must include an international cheque for $200. (This is an administration fee. The actual weapon will cost between $300 and $400, payable on delivery to your local Chinese Embassy.)

THE CHINESE PEOPLE'S REVOLUTIONARY ARMY
Foreign Affairs Division (422nd/AK-47z)
FAO Releasing Officer
Office 233/3JK
Fuxing Road
Yuyuantan Park South
Beijing

To the Releasing Officer,

Firstly, congratulations on the Communist Revolution of 1949, I hear things have gone really well since then and I look forward to visiting in the near future. I'm thinking of getting something like that started in my own country, but I'm waiting for the right moment. Currently, I am working to bring down the capitalist system from the inside.

In the meantime, I would be very grateful if you would sign the release forms for a Type 51 AK-47z Assault Rifle and ammunition so that I may procure one for the protection of myself and my family. I enclose copies of my gun ownership documents for your perusal.

I should add that I'm a great admirer of Chinese culture in general. Mao kicked butt in my book and I have seen every movie Bruce Lee ever made.

Kind Regards

▶ RIFLE TOP TIPS

▶ Find a 'secure' firing position. Ensure that no dead are within a 10-metre perimeter as the noise will bring them directly to your position. Work in pairs as per conventional snipers: one spotter and one shooter. Someone needs to guard your back as you unleash hell on the dead.

▶ Make your weapon ready and release the safety catch but do not touch the trigger until you are ready to fire.

▶ Hold the barrel area of the gun with your 'off' hand and use what support you can to steady your weapon.

▶ Place the butt of the gun in the pocket of the firing shoulder (this reduces the effect of recoil and ensures a steady position) and tilt your head so that your target eye is looking straight down the barrel and sight.

▶ As the dead stagger into view, pick your target and gently squeeze the trigger. Short bursts of 1–3 rounds are recommended. Target the upper body and head. If you are an inexperienced or nervous shooter, target the lower body.

▶ Control your breathing and match your fire pattern to the natural respiratory pause as you exhale.

▶ Never fire on fully automatic as experience has shown that more than 90% of shots will miss the target.

ZOMBIE AIMING TARGET

When using an assault rifle on single shot settings from a distance of 100–200m

Skilled Marksmen
Head shot – Kill
76% ACCURACY

Experienced Shooter
Upper Torso/Head
76% ACCURACY

Trained Newbie
Stomach/Lower Body
65% ACCURACY

Untrained Shooter
Lower Body/Legs
62% ACCURACY

ZOMBIE COMBAT AND WEAPONS

SHOTGUNS

Shotguns are the ideal firearm for the zombie apocalypse. The barrel of these flexible weapons is smooth as opposed to 'rifled' and they are designed to deliver powerful blasts at short range. Most will fire ball bearings or pellets, and there are literally hundreds of variations, but modern semi-automatic shotguns such as the Franchi SPAS-12 are pretty much unbeatable as zombie-busting weapons. The tactics below are designed for use with modern shotguns. If you find yourself armed with your Grandad's old hunting double-barrel then you will need to adapt the techniques. Any shotgun will be of use, so the capabilities of the weapon just need to be understood.

CENSORED
IMAGE DEEMED TOO SHOCKING
FOR PUBLICATION

TACTIC 1
CONTROLLED SPRAY

A controlled spray is the maintenance of ongoing but regulated fire into a horde of zombies. Typically, it is used when retreating back down a corridor while being chased by significant and tightly packed numbers of the dead. The shooter effectively walks backwards, spraying various angles of fire into the oncoming horde and switching between low and high shots. In some cases, the shooter will actually shout 'low' when aiming into the legs – the ghouls hit by the spray aren't necessarily killed but do stumble and fall, causing an obstruction to those that follow. For the other shot, the shooter will shout 'high' – this is the killer head shot designed to thin out the zombies. Behind the shotgun shooter is a fighter pulling them slowly backwards and directing them to the exit. This move requires experience, discipline and a trusted partner as the shooter is entirely occupied with maintaining the field of fire while they are led by their partner to safety.

TACTIC 2
THE SHOTGUN SPLATTER

This is an extravagant special move that involves putting the barrel of the shotgun into the mouth of the zombie and blasting upwards. This has become something of a cult move amongst seasoned zombie killers and they take great pride in measuring the distance of the splatter after a shot.

It is important to wear eye protection as the spray is infected, but this is a morale-boosting move for the gung-ho zombie warrior. Equally, it is important to ensure that any audience is well out of range of any splatter and ideally behind you, as they enjoy your shotgun showboating. As extravagant as this move may first appear, it is still one that guarantees a solid kill every time. Just ensure that the zombie doesn't push the barrel down its throat in any effort to reach your fingers – this would not be a good way to become infected!

FRANCHI
SPAS-12

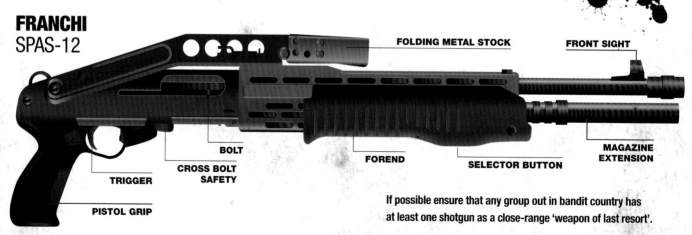

FOLDING METAL STOCK

FRONT SIGHT

BOLT

CROSS BOLT SAFETY

FOREND

SELECTOR BUTTON

MAGAZINE EXTENSION

TRIGGER

PISTOL GRIP

If possible ensure that any group out in bandit country has at least one shotgun as a close-range 'weapon of last resort'.

TACTIC 3
THE ROOM CLEARER

Clearing a building full of zombies is a nerve-wracking and dangerous process, particularly if you are unsure of its layout and the lights are out of order. However, with the right training, two experienced zombie fighters armed with shotguns can make good progress clearing locations of the dead. The first step is to have one fighter on each side of the door. They are both silent and one whistles or makes a noise to attract any ghouls within. They wait for a few seconds listening for any response. One then enters while the other covers. The fighter in the room checks each corner and any obstructions from the crouched position and shouts 'First Zombie Clear!' to indicate that the first sweep has been completed. The second fighter then enters and completes a secondary sweep covered by the first fighter, shouting 'Second Zombie Clear!' once the scan is complete. Shotguns are the perfect weapon for this kind of work.

▶ SHOTGUN TOP TIPS

▶ Wear protective clothing including face, eye and ear protectors. The blast in a confined space can be very noisy and there is a good chance of infected material splattering everywhere.

▶ Practise swinging the shotgun into the firing position in front of the mirror. Use hard-man phrases to add to the impact such as 'You lookin' at me?' or 'Do you feel lucky punk?'

▶ Remain calm in close combat. An overrun home can be a chaotic place. Always identify your target before shooting, don't just open fire at the first movement.

▶ When pointing the gun, always focus on the target, not the barrel of the gun. With a shotgun, it's a question of pointing not aiming.

▶ The shotgun is a zombie survival weapon rather than a 'kill as many as you can' weapon. It is ideal to use during a fighting retreat in an overrun location or wherever zombies are packed tightly together.

▶ If you are armed with an old-fashioned double-barrel or have limited shells then give the weapon to one of your most trusted fighters with the brief that they should only open fire when the team is in danger of being overrun.

WHY ZOMBIES DON'T LIKE SHOTGUNS

Below is an illustration of a shotgun blast slowed to 1/1,000,000th of a second. The wadding separating and splitting of the shell into 'pellets' can be seen clearly. It's these projectiles, which scatter over a decent range, that do the damage. It only needs a few to rip into a zombie skull and do the necessary damage.

STAGE 2

As the shell breaks up and splinters, you have a good balance of impact and shrapnel to do some serious damage. Even a small fast moving ball bearing can take down a zombie.

STAGE 1

Apart from a deliberate move such as the Shotgun Splatter, you should never hit a zombie this close. The shell has yet to splinter and there is a danger that the first zombie takes the full force of the blast.

STAGE 3

The most likely outcome of a shotgun blast from 15 metres upwards is to knock any zombies in the fire zone to the floor. Depending on the weapon, the power of the shot can be significantly reduced at ranges of above 30 metres.

ZOMBIE COMBAT AND WEAPONS

MACHINE GUNS

Light machine guns are typically designed to be fired by a single mobile survivor whereas medium and heavy guns typically are meant to be fired from a fixed position, say on a tripod, or rely on a second survivor to feed in a belt and for general support. Whatever the type, in the hands of a skilled operator and in the right position, these weapons can inflict some awesome destruction on advancing zombie hordes.

MACHINE GUN TACTICS FOR BEGINNERS

To defend against zombie attack, machine guns are best placed at key points in your home, for example, in prepared machine gun pits with clear views and overlapping fields of fire. The ideal strategy is to draw in the dead by offering a direct route to get to their feast. Obstacles and pits can be used to tangle and ensnare the walking dead, but the main objective is to drive them into a 'cone of death' where both gunners can concentrate their fire on a wall of rotting flesh.

Crews should be made up of the most experienced survivors. They must be disciplined enough to hold their fire until a horde attack and even then to maintain a controlled-burst fire pattern as the dead advance. Most machine guns will overheat under sustained firing so their role will be to thin out the zombie ranks as they approach. Machine guns in fortified emplacements should always be supported by other more mobile fighters.

If you have a spare machine gun, you may consider mounting it on the back of a pickup truck. This can offer your forces mobile fire support plus a cool 'bandit king' look, which will put off most human raiders. A white or red pickup truck is best for this. Black or silver ones just look cheap and will appear like you're trying too hard.

M60
MACHINE GUN

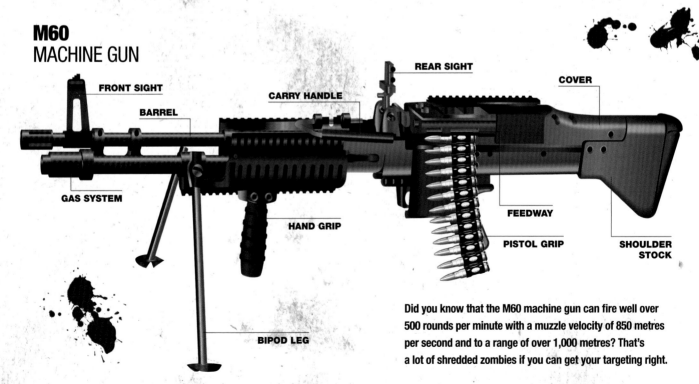

FRONT SIGHT

BARREL

CARRY HANDLE

REAR SIGHT

COVER

GAS SYSTEM

HAND GRIP

FEEDWAY

PISTOL GRIP

SHOULDER STOCK

BIPOD LEG

Did you know that the M60 machine gun can fire well over 500 rounds per minute with a muzzle velocity of 850 metres per second and to a range of over 1,000 metres? That's a lot of shredded zombies if you can get your targeting right.

▶ FIREARMS ARE NOT FOR EVERYONE

AVAILABILITY

When the zombie attack comes, it should be noted that laws concerning firearms use and ownership mean that weaponry will not be readily available to many fighters, especially in most of Europe. The chart below provides some country-by-country information on firearm availability and has been prepared by a panel of international firearms experts and the G.A.G.M. (Global Association of Gun Manufacturers), though the comments are all our own work. However, we would not advise people to move to a particular country purely because of availability of firearms. To calculate a truer 'zombie survival index' you must factor in conditions such as population density, the capacity of the local armed forces and geographical location. When these are included, countries such as Canada and Australia are good options for survival. People in the UK and Japan, though, will have a much tougher time of it.

AMMUNITION AND SPARE PARTS

Any guns in your group are only as good as the training people have had, how long the ammunition lasts and how the weapons have been maintained. If you have gathered a large survival group around you, it may be an idea to create a central armoury where stocks can be managed and weapons serviced. A knowledgeable expert can also help offer training and ensure that the right weapon is taken for the right job. For example, one survivor may be jealously clutching their prize shotgun as they do guard duty, but the weapon could be of more use to a team engaged in foraging operations. If you are preparing to survive with an extended team, it makes sense to agree a list of preferred weapons rather than have everyone picking from the thousands of variants available. The AK-47Z is ideal if you can get hold of a small batch and we strongly recommend at least one M60 machine gun.

COUNTRY	GUNS PER 100 RESIDENTS	RANK	EXPERT ANALYSIS
UNITED STATES	88.9	1	Almost a gun for every fighter. Yee-hah!
SWITZERLAND	46.3	3	Neutral, my butt – the Swiss are ready to rock and they have the cheese to back it up.
IRAQ	37.3	8	Near war conditions may be a downer on your survival plans. Don't book an airline ticket just yet.
NORWAY	33.4	11	Fjords, wonderful patterned jumpers and enough guns to start a small war. A perfect balance.
GERMANY	30.4	15	You cannot help but be disappointed. They used to have a huge arms industry but it all went so very wrong.
MONTENEGRO	25.1	21	If we knew where this was, we would pass comment. It's bound to be hot. Probably nice food as well.
ANGOLA	17.6	34	Disappointing. Very disappointing. It's like they can't be bothered.
BRAZIL	8.3	75	Perfect jungle hiding locations but no guns and lots of snakes.
UNITED KINGDOM	5.5	88	Battling the dead with a cricket bat and an unarmed police force. Classy but ineffective in terms of guns.
JAPAN	So low it doesn't show up...	171	What happened Japan? You used to be cool. Now all you have is Manga and no guns.

ZOMBIE COMBAT AND WEAPONS

THE BOW

Forget running round the forest in green tights and a small leafy hat; a modern bow is a deadly weapon in trained hands and one that could enable you to deal quickly and silently with those pesky ghouls that just won't stop hanging around. Obviously a head shot is the ideal, but this won't always be easy on a moving target or in the heat of battle. The next best target is the torso, not only because of its size but also because it is perfect for pinning a zombie to, say, a door or wall.

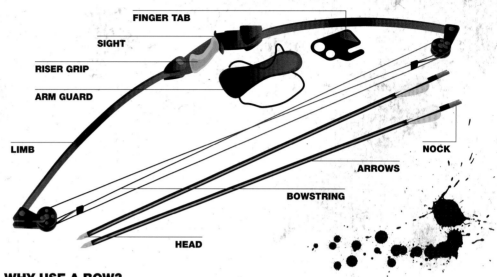

FINGER TAB
SIGHT
RISER GRIP
ARM GUARD
LIMB
NOCK
ARROWS
BOWSTRING
HEAD

WHY USE A BOW?

A bow is a flexible shaft, which is drawn back via the tension in a bow string. It is designed to fire projectiles known as arrows. There are hundreds of different types, but most modern bows are of strong, flexible fibreglass construction and come with a range of extras from stabilising systems to telescopic sights. The main advantage of a bow is its ability to 'kill' the walking dead silently, without giving away either your position or that of other survivors.

▶ HOW TO KILL A ZOMBIE USING A BOW AND ARROW

Virtually anyone can fire off an arrow from a bow, but few can do so accurately enough to hit a zombie in the head at distances of 50m or more. The bow is a weapon that requires long hours of practice and dedication to master, but with time it can become a powerful and deadly weapon in your anti-zombie arsenal. Always ensure that you carry a supporting melee weapon when you are out with a bow, even if you have support fighters around you.

STEP 1
CONFIRM TARGET

Confirm the target with your dominant eye. You need to assess factors such as distance and wind speed before preparing for your shot. Ensure that you have the right kit including an arm guard and quiver to store your arrows.

STEP 2
TAKE AIM

Ensure that you are in the correct stance. You should be comfortable but with a firm hand on the weapon and using your back muscles as an anchor point. Use three fingers to pull back the arrow in the split-finger style.

CLASS	PROJECTILE ACTION	RESULT	OUTCOME	ACTION REQUIRED
A FULL HEAD SHOT	Projectile enters through any part of the head.	80% plus of the zombie brain destroyed.	Zombie is out of action.	No follow up action required, just a smug grin.
B GLANCING HEAD SHOT	Projectile hits the head but not centrally.	Less than 80% of the zombie brain destroyed.	Zombie will recoil and may fall under the impact but is still dangerous and mobile.	This zombie will require a further projectile or follow-up with a hand weapon to kill.
C ZOMBIE PINNED	Projectile pierces a bodypart and pins the zombie down.	No damage to the brain.	The zombie struggles to move. If the hit is sufficient, the creature may end up tearing a limb or arm off in its efforts to stagger on.	A pin shot reduces the mobility of a zombie, but further action will be required to dispatch it.
D BODY HIT	Projectile pierces the chest or stomach in comic fashion.	No damage to the brain.	The projectile may or may not impede movement, but the creature is still very much a threat.	This zombie will require a further projectile or to be taken out with a hand weapon.
E COMPLETE MISS	Projectile misses the target.	No damage to the brain. Let's just hope you didn't hit any survivors.	In most cases, zombies will not 'clock' the appearance of projectile weapons. They could well ignore it and continue on.	A degree of embarrassment, followed by hours of rigorous practice with your weapon.

STEP 3
FIRE

Hold the bow arm towards your zombie target and aim down the spine of the arrow. Use a sight if you have one fitted. Release the arrow by relaxing the fingers, ensuring that the action is a as smooth as possible.

STEP 4
ASSESS KILL

Assess your kill using the Ministry of Zombies categorisation system above and determine your next action. Where possible, retrieve your arrow when it is safe to do so and remember to always carry a hand weapon for close combat.

IMPROVING ACCURACY
- Join your local archery club.
- Get the right kit and get expert advice on the right bow for you.
- Wear green if you really think it helps.
- As you gain experience, you will need to practise against moving targets. This is not something most clubs will offer. One idea is to have a zombie target on wheels and someone to pull it from side to side as you take your shot.

ZOMBIE COMBAT AND WEAPONS

THE CROSSBOW

Over recent years, the crossbow has become the weapon of choice for the many zombie survivalists around the world who have no access to firearms. Global sales from the world's top five manufacturers of modern crossbows have increased 43% and this is attributed at least in part to fears of a zombie apocalypse. Easier to master than a bow, new models are now quick to reload and many are equipped with optical scopes.

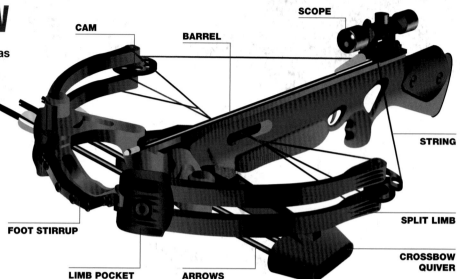

CAM
BARREL
SCOPE
STRING
SPLIT LIMB
CROSSBOW QUIVER
FOOT STIRRUP
LIMB POCKET
ARROWS

▶ THE SILENT KILL – USING A CROSSBOW AGAINST THE DEAD

A modern crossbow will be equipped with a safety catch. A cocked crossbow which is locked will obviously be more ready for use.

Fighters using ranged weapons should always be armed with a secondary melee weapon for hand-to-hand combat.

Always be aware of the wind direction when approaching the dead by stealth. Zombies have a keen sense of smell so stay down wind if possible. The best strategy with a crossbow is to make targeted kills such as taking out a zombie which happens to be blocking your way ahead. It will take time to reload so ensure that any noise you make doesn't attract more of the dead. As with every ranged weapon, get to know how the different weather conditions will affect your shot, particularly the wind and rain. Finally, ensure that you maintain your weapon. This means regular cleaning of the barrel groove in particular and try to gather up your bolts where you can as precision replacements will be very hard to make.

ACCESSORIES

▶ A poncho (not the theme park plastic ones given on water rides), an authentic Mexican chequered one.
▶ A Chopper bike (motorbike not a chopper bicycle).
▶ A shoot-from-the-hip hillbilly attitude.
▶ Optional leather waistcoat.

STEP 1
CONFIRM TARGET

Creeping through the trees, the fighter is planning on a silent kill to prevent the other creatures around 'clocking' his presence. Pause before firing to help control the breathing. A short rest of a few seconds is advised. Crossbows are very susceptible to any shaking or movement and this will misdirect the bolt.

> **THERE IS NO DOUBT THAT THE CROSSBOW IS NOW SEEN AS THE STANDARD FOR ZOMBIE SURVIVALISTS AND ALL OF OUR SALES FIGURES POINT TO PEOPLE WANTING TO BE PREPARED, WITH A WEAPON THEY CAN REALLY TRUST.**

MIKE ALDERSON, CEO CENTURY WEAPONS LTD

Many modern crossbow bolts will rip right through a brittle zombie skull, tearing chunks of the rotting grey brain matter as it passes through.

However, the zombie-specific ZK-100 bolt is designed with a bulge just after the point so that that once the tip pierces, the bulge follows into the zombie brain, causing far more damage than a regular bolt. It is estimated that a ZK-100 bolt will inflict 61% more brain damage than a standard bolt – that's significantly more zombie-busting power.

OTHER RANGED WEAPONS

A ranged weapon can deal with a zombie from a distance greater as opposed to a melee or hand weapon, which requires close combat. These weapons are a safe way to deal with the dead as you won't come anywhere near the snack radius of the zombies. However, they are, generally speaking, weapons that require more skill to operate and demand much from the user in terms of hours of practice and precision accuracy.

Weapons such as javelins and catapults are also worth investigation but again require a substantial period of training to achieve anything like the level of accuracy required to be effective. There are, however, alternatives that, under the right conditions, can be used to hit the dead from a safe distance. Dropping items such as bricks from a height is remarkably effective if you can get them on target. Where it is safe to do so, survivors under siege may start taking down a non-essential wall and engaging in what is known as 'zombie brick toss'.

STEP 2
FIRE

If it's a difficult shot, aim low and at the chest. Quickly reload, which takes 5–10 seconds for a skilled user, and deliver a second bolt to the head to finish the target. Be aware that the noise of a pin shot may attract more of the walking dead, particularly if the zombie starts groaning and tugging.

STEP 3
ASSESS KILL

Reload and return the safety catch. You are now clear to silently pass your kill. This shot can be very useful if you are escorting a party of foragers etc. Obviously, if you can retrieve the bolt then do so but do not risk a kill confirmation if it is unsafe to do so.

ZOMBIE COMBAT AND WEAPONS

MELEE WEAPONS

Many zombie survivalists view their hand held or melee weapon as the single most important piece of kit they have. It's something that is always within reach and is carried whether they are out on patrol or within a secure 'green zone' perimeter. It's the human ability to use a hand weapon that can really give you the edge in this battle for survival so soak up the knowledge over the next few pages and consider your choices carefully. Some desperate people will face the zombie apocalypse with whatever weapon happens to be around – it could be a rolling pin, a garden tool or even a small branch. However, those

planning to survive a plague of the walking dead have a chance to plan and think things through – to get something with the right weight, something durable and something that is going to save lives when the zombies come knocking.

Few countries have restrictions on melee weapons you can keep around the home but it will no doubt worry most local police forces if you start to purchase large quantities of machetes or swords. It is well-worth going along to your nearest police stations and explaining your zombie concerns – you'll be surprised how many officers are worried about the same thing.

▶ EVERYDAY HAND WEAPONS & LOCATIONS

The typical home is bristling with weapons you can use to defend yourself against both the dead and looters. However, pre-warned is pre-armed, so don't find yourself scrabbling through the kitchen drawer looking for a potato peeler – prepare now! Here are some useful ideas for weapons you can find around most homes. Be creative, once you start looking you'll find weapons everywhere – that heavy wooden tray may be a useful clubbing weapon, maybe you could take one of them out with Granny's wooden leg. Look around with fresh eyes. Do the same thing at the office or school and make a mental list of any potential weapons.

THE CAR

Caught on the road during a zombie crisis? Fear not, your vehicle is the perfect battering ram. Maintain a reasonable speed and go for glancing side blows to the dead rather than clean up and over the bonnet ramming. As for melee weapons, car doors are perfect whacking weapons.

KEY ITEM

A quality tyre iron is a great zombie-bashing tool. There are some drawbacks in terms of length, but in the first desperate hours it will get the job done.

THE GARAGE

Grab a baseball, cricket or any decent sports bat and you'll have a real fighting chance. Forget golf clubs as they tend to bend on first contact. Add nails to give your weapon that extra zip. A well-stocked garage is a veritable treasure trove of weapons against the dead so make sure you're first to the hammer.

KEY ITEM

With perfect balance, a purpose-made handle and smooth action, few melee weapons beat a cricket or baseball bat. You can add nails or barbed wire to 'spice up' your weapon.

PREPARATION FOR THE DESPERATE

If you are reading this and the zombies are slobbering at your window then it's safe to assume you have become a believer. Here's what you should spend the next hours doing:

1 SECURE YOUR LOCATION – your first action should be to close and lock all downstairs windows and doors. Once this is done work around the building checking that every opening is secure.

2 GATHER YOUR SURVIVORS – get whoever is within the sealed perimeter together. Ensure they understand that the building has been sealed. If anyone wants to leave, manage their exit so that you can seal the doors after them.

3 WEAPONS – next priority is to get everyone armed with at least a basic weapon. Once you have your weapons ensure that the building is fully clear of any dead – patrol in pairs if you can.

4 WATER AND FOOD – there is a great deal of water trapped in various systems around most buildings so locate any tanks and isolate them. It is a good idea to have another survivor collecting all the food together. Start rationing from the moment you are sealed in.

5 JUST SURVIVING – If you have the supplies then convince the rest of your party to stay put for at least the short-term. If you assess your location and it's hopeless then you may need to move but it is safer to stay where you are if you can. Ensure that you have a guard posted at all times and start to think through your survival plans. If you can dig out your old Haynes manual then do it.

THAT MIGHT GET YOU THROUGH THE FIRST FEW WEEKS OF A MAJOR ZOMBIE OUTBREAK BUT YOU ARE GOING TO HAVE TO LEARN FAST AND TOUGHEN UP IF YOU WANT TO SURVIVE MUCH LONGER!

THE KITCHEN

Forget the knives as these weapons will simply go through the rotting flesh of the dead. Instead, look for any heavy rolling pins or wooden cutting boards to help get you 'cooking' in the zombie-bashing business. As a last resort, you can always throw the microwave or toaster at them.

THE BEDROOM

Pull a drawer out, empty it and you have a useful one time weapon. Sheets can be used to throw over a zombie, allowing you to make an escape. A zombie attack is also the perfect opportunity to use any rubbish art you have on the wall as a weapon – it may not do much damage but at least you will be rid of it.

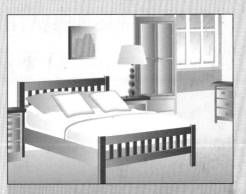

Honour any Celtic heritage by grabbing Grandad's shillelagh from the wall and hoping it isn't just a ceremonial one. Any family swords, shields or daggers could be put to good use ensuring your own survival.

KEY ITEM

An old fashioned rolling pin is as perfect for zombie bashing as is it for making delicious pastries and treats. Crack a few zombie heads then bake yourself a celebratory pie afterwards – just ensure you wash off any blood first.

KEY ITEM

A lampshade with a heavy base will make an acceptable emergency club. Always remove the electrical cord to prevent it wrapping around and tripping you. Keep the lampshade if you like the colour.

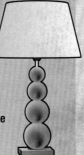

THERE'S NO NEED TO RESORT TO FLINGING YOUR PRECIOUS RECORDS IF OTHER ITEMS ARE AROUND

ZOMBIE COMBAT AND WEAPONS

WEIRD, EXOTIC AND DIY

So far we've covered some of the much-loved classics of zombie combat, from firearms to baseball bats and several cool weapons in-between; however, the zombie apocalypse will also present an opportunity to get creative with your choice of arms. So, if you've always coveted thy neighbour's powerful nail gun then now is the time to get out and buy yourself one. These amazing machines cause around 40,000 injuries around the world every year and so their reputation pretty much speaks for itself. Basically, if you have a weapon which is robust and can do the business on a zombie brain then why not innovate to use something you've designed for yourself – be it a gun firing six inch nails or specially adapted chainsaw with cool skull and cross bone markings. There are so many options out there including sledgehammers and machetes, you are really spoilt for choice.

There is also a wide range of weapons available on the internet, some of which have been designed with zombie busting in mind, such as the lead 'zombie-crusher' baseball bat from the Hero Sports Group.

THE 'WOULD-BE NINJA'

A survey completed by *Car and Gun Magazine* in the US in 2006 asked readers to recommend the ideal ranged weapon with which to fight zombies. The top answer was quite rightly the crossbow, but more than 31% of respondents reported that they had not only ordered but also practised with ninja-throwing stars in preparation for the zombie apocalypse.

WHY THROWING STARS WILL GET YOU KILLED:

▶ The chances are you are not a trained ninja and the likelihood of you hitting a zombie head with a throwing star is very slim.
▶ Even if you do hit the creature, a star will not penetrate deep enough to do any serious damage.
▶ Wearing your black pyjama outfit will look very conspicuous as you slink through the abandoned streets. You may also sweat a lot, attracting even more of the dead.

▶ FIRE AND THE DEAD

As a rule, zombies and fire don't mix. For most desiccated ghouls, even the hint of a flame seems to halt their advance. However, this rule is by no means universal. For example, starting a fire at an encampment is a great way to attract the dead – it seems that the movement or scent of the smoke just attracts them.

There are literally hundreds of ways you can attack the walking dead with fire – just remember that a burning zombie may still lumber forward. The heat of the flame needs to destroy at least 80% of the brain to take the creature down. Burn times on a classic zombie are typically 1-3 minutes – this is from the moment its head is alight to the moment it collapses. This timeframe will depend on factors such as climate and the clothing the zombie is wearing. It often surprises inexperienced zombie fighters that when they throw a petrol bomb or set a zombie on fire, the creature will frequently keep shuffling towards them, even as it is blazing away. Such creatures are called 'flamers' and you generally get flamers when the fire is on the body of the zombie rather than the head.

PETROL BOMBS

Petrol Bombs, or Molotov Cocktails, can be made easily using any flammable liquid. They are then best hurled into packs of the dead. In Ministry of Zombies tests, even larger petrol bombs did little real damage to a group of zombies. A good hit may take out one or two but they are not as effective as untrained survivors believe. Beware of the odd flaming zombie running towards your site – they have a nasty habit of spreading fires.

COMBAT AND WEAPONS
THE CLASSIC CHAINSAW

CLOSE COMBAT? NO NEED FOR QUIET?

Then embark on a death-defying slashing fest, which can hack tens of zombies into casserole chunks. That's what the mighty chainsaw offers – a powerful handheld weapon with a reputation for carnage amongst zombie fighters.

COMBAT TECHNIQUES

Combat techniques against the dead when using a chainsaw used to be based on aggressive slashing, but improvements in chainsaw technology – in particular lighter machines – have allowed a more skilful combat art to develop. Known as the 'Dance of the Chainsaw', it leans surprisingly on ballet, focusing on balance and poise when in combat. The fighter launches a series of different moves to counter any lunge made by a zombie and then returns to a well-balanced 'aplomb' position.

FLAMETHROWER

If you have one handy, the flamethrower can be a devastating weapon against the dead. Always remember to accompany each flamethrower-armed survivor with other fighters to offer protection and fire using short, controlled bursts. This weapon can be particularly useful for clearing long corridors of the dead. Always allow a few minutes for the ghouls to properly cook.

CITY OF THE DEAD FIRES

As your group starts to liberate more territory from the dead, you will doubtless come across some towns or cities which are so dangerously infested with the dead that it's easy to take out the whole site, then go building-to-building zombie clearing. It is good practice to send a vehicle with a loud speaker through the area first to warn survivors and give them time to evacuate.

ZOMBIE COMBAT AND WEAPONS

COMBAT FOR THE ELDERLY

A zombie apocalypse will be a particularly hard time for the elderly for, although they have much wisdom and many interesting stories to share, particularly about the 'good old days', few are ready to defend themselves against the walking dead. Well, that's what many think. However, UK and American charity organisation Age Zombie Awareness (AZA) has been working for over a decade and in nations across the world to prepare the elderly for a zombie outbreak. In fact, to date almost 100,000 people over the age of 65 in Europe and North America have been through basic zombie combat training, making them one of the best prepared demographic groups. The AZA training includes support with developing Bug-Out plans and food storage advice as well as actual combat training and top tips for playing bingo. The Ministry of Zombies is the AZA's only licensed partner and the following content was designed by their experts and is part of their most popular course 'Senior Citizen, Senior Survivor'.

'DANCE LIKE FRED ASTAIRE AND STING LIKE MUHAMMAD ALI!' – A FIGHTING MOTTO FROM THE AZA TRAINING COURSE

► WALKING FRAME DEFENCE TECHNIQUES FROM THE AZA COURSE

STEP 1
THE VALUE OF A HEARING AID

After a foraging mission to the shops, an elderly survivor is targeted by a shuffling zombie. The creature approaches its target. Our survivor easily picks up the noise of its dragging feet by wearing an enhanced and highly sensitive hearing aid. She does not respond immediately as she is also wearing a ghoulish perfume musk which may make the zombie ignore her. No luck this time as the zombie continues to approach. She braces for action.

STEP 2
THE FOUR-PRONGED LOCK

The survivor only springs into action once the creature is within range. Once it is within a metre or so she swings her walking frame up and traps the zombie, blocking its approach. If there is a wall or fence nearby, she can pin the zombie against it. Either way, the ghoul is contained as she either calls for help or makes plans for her escape.

COMBAT WITH A WALKING STICK

The course 'Senior Citizen, Senior Survivor' includes sessions on zombie combat using everyday objects such as shopping bags, a rolled-up newspaper and even a bulky TV guide. However, a particular emphasis is placed on training for combat using a walking stick. The AZA has developed a range of walking sticks which have been adapted to include a shooting spike at the end. This spike can be released at the touch of a button on the handle and can be used to pin a zombie and keep the creature at a safe distance. Target practice sessions encourage elderly combatants to first aim for the chest before honing their skills with an accurate head shot. A jab to the head followed with a spring-loaded spike jab will dispatch most zombies.

GUNS FOR GRANNY

The organisation Age Zombie Awareness does not currently deliver a course on firearms for the elderly, but it does highlight in several pamphlets that many older people, particularly veterans of the Second World War and other conflicts, are already trained and experienced with various types of gun. In fact, pioneering work has already been completed by a group of these veterans to create a zombie-busting gun particularly for the elderly. It is based on the antique 'blunderbuss' used by an elderly Irish grandmother in Belfast in 1979. Other survivors were amused as Mrs Cassidy took aim at a group of approaching zombies but were stunned when the shot from her brass musket spread and destroyed every one of the dead. Mrs Cassidy herself had her wheeled shopping basket specially adapted to carry the weapon and additional iron pellets.

STEP 3
THE FRAME FLICK

With no other survivors in the area and more of the dead nearby, our elderly survivor does not want to call for help so she uses all of her strength to pull the walking frame back and then flick it sideways, sending the creature tumbling to the ground. She can then either deliver a walking frame stamp, which will impale one of the struts through the soft, brittle skull of the zombie, or just make her escape.

ZOMBIE COMBAT AND WEAPONS

FIXED DEFENCES

What could be better than sitting in a deckchair behind your defences hearing the pleasing snap as another zombie is caught in that mantrap you 'foraged' from the museum, or the moan as another ghoul tumbles into one of your spiked pits? Well, taking out zombies requires more focus than this.

Whether you are defending a major settlement of survivors or just going it alone in your gun shop, fixed defences can help deal with the zombies while you watch with an insane grin.

For the first weeks of a major zombie outbreak, the streets will be chaos with desperate and unprepared survivors running everywhere in search of safety. This is not the time to be leaving your carefully prepared stronghold. Stay inside during this period and 'run silent'. However, as you reach the one-month point, things will be quieter and you should consider working out some viable fixed defences to improve your set-up. For example, are there any large vehicles nearby you can use to block off roads, or ways you could extend a fence to create an additional perimeter.

Make use of any natural barriers such as rivers and don't overlook the obvious such as sealing or bricking up a house to create a large defensive barrier. You may not have the resources to dig a moat around your property so make use of what's around you to create significant zombie barriers, then augment your perimeter with some cunning traps to ensnare the walking dead.

▶ SUNKEN DEFENCES

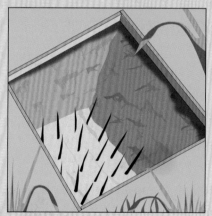

SUNKEN DEFENCE 1
THE DITCH OR HOLE

The simple ditch or any hole is an obstacle to the walking dead as they frequently lack the foresight to avoid it and the dexterity to get out. If you lack the resources for a full two-metre ditch around your home, try lifting the man-hole covers and howl with laughter as the dead tumble in. Just ensure that you don't follow them and that there are no survivors sheltering down there.

SUNKEN DEFENCE 2
THE GHOUL PIT

This is basically any hole or ditch which has been filled with obstructions to do damage to the dead. The idea is that as the zombies fall in, they are impaled on the spikes and can be dealt with at your leisure. Again, always ensure that you place a warning above such a trap. Zombies can't read so you don't need to worry about them dodging your carefully-prepared traps.

SUNKEN DEFENCE 3
THE MOAT

The last of the sunken defences. Unless you live in a 15th-century chateau, it is unlikely that your home will be surrounded by a moat. However, sensible use of a flooded ditch or river can be a useful way of securing a flank from zombie attack. Of course, the dead could always float over, but it does at least give some defence. Do not start digging a moat around your home unless you have the room and planning permission.

ZOMBIE COMBAT AND WEAPONS
MAN (ZOMBIE) TRAPS

Both the modern claymore anti-personnel mine and iron man trap are designed to wound rather than kill humans so their effect on the dead is marginal. For example, the man trap was used by landowners to fend off poachers and was banned in virtually every country. The serrated edges of the metal jaws can cut right through zombie limbs and inflict horrific wounds, but are not designed to kill. The claymore anti-personnel mine fires hundreds of ball bearings into the air but presents no particular threat to a zombie. An effective zombie trap must delay, kill or incapacitate a significant number of the dead to be useful. Targeted killing is no use.

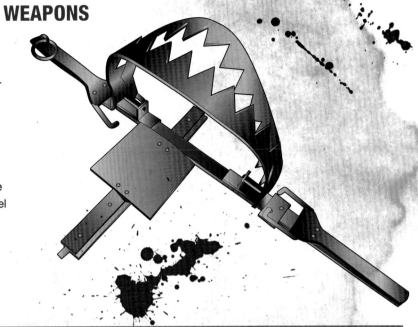

▶ SPIKED DEFENCES

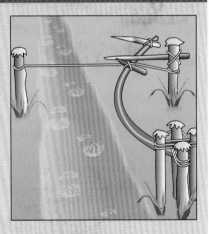

SPIKED DEFENCE 1
DEFENSIVE ARRAY

Low-tech solutions work on the dead and any spiked defences are ideal for slowing the dead down. Zombies are clumsy and will always catch themselves on any spikes or wires. Even a chord stretched across the road could cause them to stumble. Be sure to hang some form of warning on your defences. A makeshift barrier won't be a watertight perimeter and beware of any holes through which crawlers could creep.

SPIKED DEFENCE 2
RAZOR WIRE

Again, this is designed to slow zombies down as they become entangled in razor or barb wire. It can be very useful where laid in multiple layers. A horde of the walking dead will get through such a barrier eventually, but it can serve as a useful delaying tactic. If you don't have access to the real thing, any DIY store will have chicken wire or mesh which, with the addition of a few cuts and jagged edges, can be a worthy substitute.

SPIKED DEFENCE 3
TRIGGER WIRE

There are literally thousands of variations of the trigger-wire trap you can use to create effective anti-zombie fortifications. Most are spring-loaded and designed to make noise as well as take out the zombie unfortunate enough to trip them. Smaller trigger-wire traps can be used to catch small mammals such as rabbits and therefore provide a useful supplement of fresh meat.

ZOMBIE COMBAT AND WEAPONS

ZOMBIE PROFILES

Something that confuses most fighters when they first encounter the walking dead is the obvious variation. To the untrained eye it appears that there are different kinds of zombie, that the zombic condition somehow creates different symptoms in some humans and there is some truth in this. In zombiology, we call these zombie 'types' as they are in no way variations in any medical definition. They are all humans who have been transformed into ravenous walking corpses by the zombie virus. However, with factors such as climate, injury, age profile and even look, the zombie fighter can find themselves facing a variety of these different zombie types.

The Ministry of Zombies recognises seven official types of zombie although there are considerable variations and some types may be combined. Know these types, their attack vectors and how to fight them.

INFECTED HUMANS

Some zombie fighters recognise an eighth zombie type, infected humans, as although they may not have yet developed the symptoms of the zombic condition, they are still a clear danger to any living survivor. Typically these individuals know they've been infected but will do anything in their power to hide this fact from fellow survivors. Ironically, they seem drawn to survivor groups and in the short time they have left, will try to work their way into a group.

If you encounter any stray survivors you suspect of being infected you can either take them in and then keep them in a secure compound under observation for 48 hours or tell them to be on their way if you are short on supplies or suspect their motives. If you choose the latter, use the following advice:

1 Give a clear warning **'Stay back or I will use lethal force'**. Do not allow them to approach even if they insist they just want to talk. You can always throw out food and supplies if they need it.

2 Depending on the situation, you may fire a warning shot. Do not allow this individual to join your group if they have clear bite marks. If you are not going to quarantine them then they need to be either on their way or you will need to take them down.

3 Keep watching if they choose to walk away. Be wary in case they try to sneak back towards you. This is something virtually every infected survivor will do. They may hide and wait until night before trying to get into your compound. It is a sad fact that few infected humans will walk away from a human settlement.

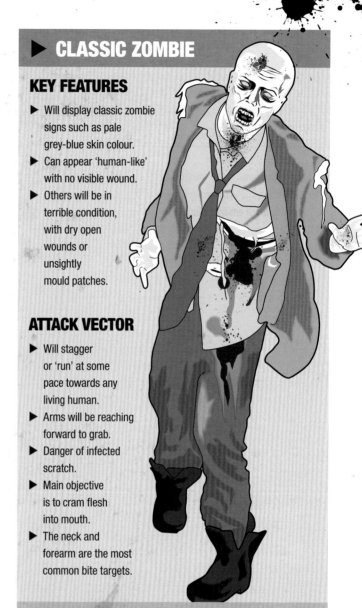

▶ CLASSIC ZOMBIE

KEY FEATURES

▶ Will display classic zombie signs such as pale grey-blue skin colour.

▶ Can appear 'human-like' with no visible wound.

▶ Others will be in terrible condition, with dry open wounds or unsightly mould patches.

ATTACK VECTOR

▶ Will stagger or 'run' at some pace towards any living human.

▶ Arms will be reaching forward to grab.

▶ Danger of infected scratch.

▶ Main objective is to cram flesh into mouth.

▶ The neck and forearm are the most common bite targets.

COMBAT STRATEGY

1 Identify the zombie (use picture if unsure). This will be an important step early on as trigger-happy survivors open fire on everything and everyone.

2 A heavy blow or shot to the head will do the business – aiming to destroy at least 80% of the brain.

3 Confirm the kill with a foot stamp or club hit. Always check your zombie kills before notching them up on your zombie kill chart.

ALL ZOMBIE TYPES ARE DANGEROUS, ALL CAN KILL BUT SOME ARE MORE DEADLY THAN OTHERS

▶ BLOATERS

KEY FEATURES

▶ Bulky and over-sized zombies, bloated by the build-up of acid and gas within the corpse.

▶ Humid and tropical conditions mean that this excess liquid builds pressure within the zombie, particularly in the stomach and intestines.

▶ Bloaters can be very dangerous in confined spaces and are prone to block entire corridors.

ATTACK VECTOR

▶ A bloater has the same flesh-feeding instinct as any other zombie.

▶ Its bulk makes it a slow opponent and an easy target.

▶ It stumbles towards targets.

▶ If it trips, it can suffocate opponents in folds of putrid and rotting flesh.

▶ It is prone to necromesis – the ejecting of stomach acid and bile at velocity.

▶ In confined spaces, bloaters will use their lumbering bulk to block escape routes.

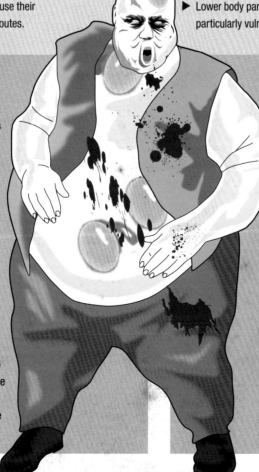

COMBAT STRATEGY

1 Never shoot or pierce a bloater at close range. These creatures are full of pressurised bile and infected vomit. They will explode if punctured.

2 Create distance between yourself and a bloater with a strong two handed shove. Alternatively, a double drop kick when it is safe to do so.

3 After creating aforementioned distance (you need at least 3 metres), aim a shot, arrow or spear towards the head of the creature. If you can leave the body then do, but if you need to deflate it then a long hollow pole shoved into the side of the creature will allow the pressure to be released safely.

▶ KIDDIE GHOULS

KEY FEATURES

▶ Children are infected with the zombie virus in the same way as adults.

▶ The conversion process is slightly faster in children under 16.

▶ Kiddie ghouls tend to be faster and more dextrous than the adult zombie due to their growing muscle mass.

ATTACK VECTOR

▶ The right kiddie ghoul can reduce even the most seasoned zombie fighter to inaction.

▶ These creatures use that second of uncertainty to race forward at pace.

▶ Their zones of attack are all below the belt.

▶ Lower body parts are therefore particularly vulnerable.

COMBAT STRATEGY

1 Be prepared for the harrowing sight of a ten-year-old zombie. It's tragic, but never forget they are the undead and should be destroyed in the same way as adult zombies.

2 Be cautious of kicking these tiny terrors. Even experienced fighters are prone to miss these fast moving creatures, allowing them to sink their teeth into the flesh or kneecap of the defender.

3 If you are armed, take your time as you will typically only get one shot and remember, when under stress shoot low. The idea is to stop the creature. A head shot is hard on kiddie ghouls.

4 If you are unarmed then time your kick as the creature is just about to reach you. Aim it towards the chest to avoid it being knocked over by your kick and into your body.

ZOMBIE COMBAT AND WEAPONS

▶ LIMBLESS WONDERS

KEY FEATURES

- ▶ A zombie that has been through some trauma and has its arms severed.
- ▶ Limbless wonders tend to be quicker than full-bodied zombies due to their reduced body weight.
- ▶ They have fewer attack options than other zombies, with no grabbing hands.

ATTACK VECTOR

- ▶ Limbless wonders will run straight at you.
- ▶ They tend to dash at almost human-like speed.
- ▶ Their only objective is to rush forward and bury their jaws into your flesh.
- ▶ They often tilt their head down in a headbutt manoeuvre before their final attack.
- ▶ Where a creature's limbs have been severed below the elbow, be cautious as the stumps tend to be sharp and jagged, making them very effective slashing weapons in combat.

COMBAT STRATEGY

1. When armed these creatures are easily dealt with, but when unarmed and caught unaware by a limbless wonder, always secure your balance first. If the creature is very close, you can risk a quick dodge with your foot left out and the attacking zombie will trip and be sent crashing to the floor.
2. A powerful jumping kick or two-handed shove to the zombie's chest will unbalance it and send it the floor.
3. Follow up with a trusty stamp to the head. Generally, once they are on the ground, limbless wonders struggle to get up.

▶ CRAWLERS

KEY FEATURES

- ▶ Zombies with both legs missing are known as crawlers.
- ▶ These creatures tend to be very degraded due to their ground-hugging 'lifestyle'.
- ▶ Crawlers are a particularly harrowing sight and may have entrails such as intestines dragging behind them.

ATTACK VECTOR

- ▶ Crawlers move by dragging themselves along the ground with their jagged fingers.
- ▶ They can squeeze through the smallest holes in fences or gates and are prone to surprise the unprepared.
- ▶ They are mostly noiseless as they lay horizontal and typically attack the lower leg.

COMBAT STRATEGY

1. Sensible footwear should be worn. High boots will offer some protection from the grab or bite of an unseen crawler.
2. Where a crawler is visible, they can be easily dealt with most safely by impaling them with a long spear. This way you don't need to go close to the creature.
3. Where you are surprised by a crawler, leap into the air as soon as you notice it and aim to come down squarely with both feet, in what is known as a 'superstamp', to cave in the skull of the crawler. Do not attempt this manoeuvre in flip-flops. Sensible footwear is advisable whenever you face zombies in combat.

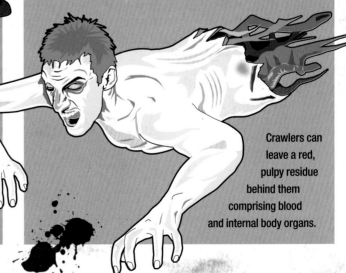

Crawlers can leave a red, pulpy residue behind them comprising blood and internal body organs.

▶ SEVERED HEADS

KEY FEATURES

▶ Zombie heads can survive when severed from the body for weeks.

▶ Zombiology does not yet understand how these isolated heads 'live'.

▶ The zombie has very little movement, but it has been known to move by wriggling its jaws along the ground.

ATTACK VECTOR

▶ Severed zombie heads have only one vector of attack.

▶ They will try to take a bite out of any foot or leg that comes close enough.

▶ They are capable of reaching forward a few inches but no more.

▶ Where they become trapped in trees or on shelves, they can drop onto the unwary, taking a chunk of flesh as they fall.

COMBAT STRATEGY

1 If you find a zombie head in the open then take the chance to improve the morale of your group by trying to deal with it creatively. Firstly, approach the head with good balance and a firm footing.

2 Swing leg with force and make sure you get a good connection with the football sized head.

3 Scream goal as you run back to your group, waving your hands in the air or perhaps removing a garment and swinging it around your head wildly. Be sure that you are not kicking any severed head zombie or 'snapper' into another group of humans.

Alternatively, you could just stick a knife into the top of the skull to deal with a stray head. Always be careful to stay out of snapping range so ensure that you use a long blade. Don't go trying it with a pen knife as you will need to bury it deep within the brain to do the job.

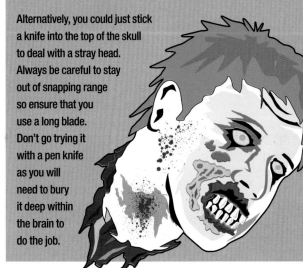

▶ SEDUCTIVE ZOMBIES

KEY FEATURES

▶ Some zombies can appear almost 'attractive' to living survivors.

▶ The world of the celebrity will be hit hard by the zombie virus.

▶ Survivors may be confused or distracted when coming face to face with one of these seductive-but-deadly creatures.

ATTACK VECTOR

▶ A seductive zombie will attack, the same as any other ghoul.

▶ It may 'learn' something of the distracting effect it has on survivors and use this as a hunting technique.

▶ Expect prolonged eye-to-eye contact before teeth-to-flesh munching activity begins.

COMBAT STRATEGY

1 If you encounter any of our beloved reality TV stars – open fire. Forget the 'identify as a zombie' or warning stage – just fire. Chances are they are zombies.

2 Avoid eye contact with these beguiling creatures. They have no supernatural power, but they can draw you in.

3 Blast the creature as quickly as possible. A direct head shot with a shotgun is best to destroy any lingering good looks.

Some fighters insist that female zombies use the long, lingering stare more whereas moody, lank hair male zombies, attempt a more brooding look.

OUT AND ABOUT IN ZOMBIE TOWN

Whether you're foraging in a nearby house for supplies or relocating to a safer long-term location, there will be many occasions during the zombie apocalypse when you need to leave your fortified home and head out into zombie town.

Make no mistake, any transport in 'bandit country' will be dangerous and any human movement will attract the attention of the dead. If you are well prepared and have your full 90-day supplies sorted and stored then you shouldn't need to venture outside of your secure base for weeks. However, it's still a good idea to have a quick scout around on about Day 50 to survey your immediate area. Start by observing from a high vantage point such as a loft window, then check out some nearby homes. If you are in an area of low zombie density, use this as a chance to stock up on any supplies you find and join up with other survivors. During your initial forays into zombie town, travel light and stay close to your home base. By Day 70, you should have completed a serious assessment of your current location and immediate area. It's then time to decide whether you move on or develop a settlement where you are.

THE ZOMBIE TRAVEL SAFETY CODE

Regardless of how you are travelling, learn the Zombie Travel Safety Code and always consider it before you travel. This code was developed by the US government in the 1980s but was never used due to concerns over public opinion. They even went as far as designing a Zombie Safety character known as the 'Zombie Safety Chameleon' which was meant to educate people about zombie safety and 'staying hidden' from the dead. Many of the key points are instinctive to experienced zombie fighters. For example, staying silent when moving and first contact protocols. However, the code has gone on to form the basis of virtually all zombie survival training. It is important that you maintain a good level of alertness when out foraging or on patrol in zombie town and it is recommended that you are never more than three hours away from a secure base. As a final pointer, be careful to avoid picking up a straggler – that is a shambling zombie who picks up your scent and staggers after you but can't catch up.

OUT AND ABOUT IN ZOMBIE TOWN
FORAGING – IS IT STEALING?

Your 90-day survival plan is designed to give you a fighting chance in the zombie apocalypse. It hopefully means you won't need to go out desperately searching for a tin of peaches and ironically getting yourself eaten looking for something to eat.

In 2009, and promoted by a series of natural disasters, the United Nations in New York issued the following clarification on emergency foraging in disaster areas:

▶ Survivors may make reasonable use of the resources around them providing they are neither in use nor claimed by another survivor.
▶ Survivors may not hoard excessive quantities of food, water or resources and may not profiteer from their collection.
▶ Any weapons of mass destruction are excluded from this declaration.

Basically, as long as the property is clearly abandoned and there are no other survivors there, it's 'help yourself'.

ON ANY FORAGING MISSION make a list of what you are after and don't be tempted to overload with stock you don't need. Target the essentials first and work to keep your 90-day stock topped up. If you encounter armed survivors who claim the supplies as their own, back away as there should be plenty for everyone in the first year of the zombie apocalypse. It is best to avoid the well-known locations in the first months of the crisis. Supermarkets, gun shops and shopping centres will become the focus for various unsavoury gangs of looters and thieves. The best scenario is if you can find one of those large white supermarket warehouses that tend to sit on the edge of town. Many of these buildings look like any other warehouse but inside you'll find enough food and supplies to feed a small army for years. If you manage to secure one of these locations, it may be worth considering it as a long-term settlement location rather than trying to move all of the stocks.

NEVER LEAD A ZOMBIE BACK TO YOUR HOME BASE OR YOU RISK ATTRACTING MORE OF THE WALKING DEAD

▶ THE ZOMBIE TRAVEL SAFETY CODE

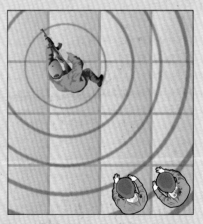

STEP 1
EXIT

Always check the coast is clear before exiting a door or your vehicle. A quick scan will normally suffice and don't forget to look behind you. Use hand signals to communicate with fellow survivors and keep noise to a minimum.

STEP 2
BE READY

It's basic: have a version of your Bug-Out Bag and a weapon, and know where your safe locations are. It does mean you won't be able to carry as many supplies when foraging but safety first! Remember that a balanced Bug-Out Bag will be your only lifeline.

STEP 3
SCANNING

Keep your eyes regularly scanning the environment – never stare too long at one building or site. Zombies can be surprisingly quiet so maintain that 360-degree scan every few minutes. When out walking on patrol, always conduct a 360-degree sweep every 20 metres.

STEP 4
LANDSCAPE

Know your enemy, always look for hidden corners where they are likely to lurk. Clock alternative routes and take in as much about the surrounding area as possible. Be cautious, get to know the area well and stay alive.

STEP 5
FIRST CONTACT

Hide, take out or run – these are options that you need to quickly weigh up. If there is just one zombie, maybe it can be dealt with quietly. If there is a small horde, maybe it is time to retreat coolly out of danger.

STEP 6
AWARENESS

Don't allow your guard to drop for a second. This makes time outside the settlement tiring so ensure you make best use of it and stay somewhere safe overnight. Experienced fighters call this 'staying frosty'.

OUT AND ABOUT IN ZOMBIE TOWN

WALKING IN A WORLD OF THE DEAD

Travelling long distances on foot will be the norm in a world dominated by zombies. Sure, it would be safer going by car, but with blocked roads, burnt-out buildings and collapsed bridges in many cases travel by foot will be the only way. Even when you can use a vehicle, there will be times when you need to leave it to forage within a building or to reach a trapped survivor elsewhere. Your fitness regime will help ensure you have the fortitude for long walks, but here are some guidelines to help you prepare for the pleasures of walking in zombie town. In terms of preparation, start with long walks as part of your training and try to complete at least one 6 to 8-mile walk on top of your normal physical training.

Just remember that you will only move as fast as your slowest survivor. So, if you have the elderly or people overloaded with supplies, you will not only be slower, you may also lose the dynamic ability to respond to zombie attacks. Our main advantage over the dead is our speed and agility – don't negate these or you risk getting eaten.

FEEL THE NEED FOR SPEED?

Assuming you don't have access to a car or that the roads are so choked that you can't get off the drive, there are still some alternatives to travelling on foot but you should always take into account that high speed travel and zombies don't mix well! Here are a few modes you may want to consider:

▶ **BICYCLES** – a decent mountain bike could be a great way to get around once the zombies arrive. You can add panniers to carry supplies in and you would easily be able to out run any zombies.

▶ **ROLLER SKATES** – are you insane? Unless you are a skilful skater – the type that parades around the park in a crop top during summer doing sweeping spins, be very cautious of donning your leotard and skates because of the sheer lack of control.

▶ **MOTORCYCLES** – now we are talking – just imagine surviving the end of the world on a cool chopper bike with your weapons strapped on your back. An all-terrain motorbike would be required not just a street racer.

▶ MRS WOODFORD'S ZOMBIE GUIDE TO DOGS

Legendry British canine expert, Mrs Victoria Woodford, created the following guide in the 1970s to help you prepare your beloved pet for the zombie apocalypse. At the time, little was known about the virus but Mrs Woodford knew the value of a loyal companion and quickly realised that our furry friends may be of great service when the dead rise.

STEP 1
TRAINING TO SMELL

Train your dog to smell zombies by finding a rotting body part and make the dog familiar with the smell. Do not be alarmed if the animal nibbles it, they will not develop the zombic condition.

STEP 2
SMELLING THE DEAD

Now hide a dead zombie and see if the dog can find it. Use short phrases such as 'where's the zombie boy?' to alert the dog that they must scan for the telltale scent of a walking corpse.

CORRECT FOOTWEAR

Believe it or not, a good pair of broken-in walking boots could save your life.
If you start to slow down with blisters then you will become a target for any dead in the area.

TRAINING IS IMPORTANT

You should be able to complete up to a five-hour trek per day and be able to sustain this for up to five days. This is a general guide but should be your target in your fitness training.

EARLY STARTS

Try to get started as soon as there is daylight. Darkness is not your friend as zombies have an excellent sense of smell and the lack of light will make your walking route more dangerous.

SNACK RADIUS

Be aware of your snack radius at all times. Keep to the middle of roads where you can and away from blind corners or trees. This can help minimise the risk of a zombie clawing out from nowhere.

EYES AROUND

Every few minutes or so, carry out a slow turn as you walk to scan 360 degrees to check whether there are any zombies who may be stumbling after you. This is a well-known military patrol technique.

ALWAYS BE ARMED

Never be without your weapon. Trekking poles have proved to be very poor when it comes to bashing zombies as many are now made of light fibreglass.

BUG-OUT BAG

Carry a scaled down version of your Bug-Out Bag, even if you are just out foraging. Be equipped with the essentials you need to survive for 24–48 hours away from your main site.

RUN AND HIDE

If you are cornered or become trapped while out walking, find a safe place to hold up and run silent. If necessary, this could involve you running silent for up to 48 hours so take a book in your pack.

THE RIGHT PACING

The average zombie will not be able to keep up at only a brisk walk and it will conserve your energy. If you exhaust yourself, the dead will just keep coming and you could be overwhelmed.

STEP 3
WALKIES FOR THE DEAD

Experiment with some brisk walks in areas where you know there are rotting corpses. Ensure that you pass within yards of the rotting bodies and allow your canine to pick up the scent and alert you to their presence.

STEP 4
OUT AND ABOUT

Now when the zombies arrive you will be ready. Remember to carry a firearm and continue to congratulate your dog on each 'spot' they make. Be aware that in areas covered with the dead, the strong scent may confuse your dog.

Canines are by far the best pets to train for anti-zombie work and it is rumoured that the Chinese Red Army makes extensive use of specially bred Chow Chow dogs to support their anti-zombie patrols. These dogs are not used to attack the dead, simply to alert their human partners that the undead are near. To date, only dogs have proved capable of anti-zombie activity although there is some interesting work being done in Northern England with ferrets.

FIRST-CONTACT PROTOCOLS

After the initial carnage of the zombie apocalypse and as you move outside for the first time, you and your fellow survivors must have a clear set of protocols for dealing with the various individuals and groups you will encounter, including other survivors, zombies and even wild animals. Remember, society will have changed – you will need to change your mind set to match a new and much harsher reality.

INDIVIDUALS AND SMALL GROUPS

The golden rule of the zombie wasteland is to never trust anyone. Sounds harsh but the various scavengers and bandits you meet as you forage for supplies will be desperate and you shouldn't take any chances. Be polite and clear where you can but always back it up with force. Never appear vulnerable and be wary of any tricks designed to make you drop your guard. Basically, you should treat any individual or small group you encounter with caution. In the early days, things can be more informal but as your survivor group grows you will need to adopt strict policies to integrate any new people into your group.

LARGER GROUPS

Here are some first-contact protocols for dealing with any new group of survivors.

1 Always try to 'encounter' groups away from your main site. This will be mean scouting and search patrols. Better to assess them at a neutral location than at your own front door.

2 On first contact, be firm and steady; carefully assess the group's capabilities and intent. Most will be scared, embattled families just looking to survive.

3 It may be an idea to create a meeting point at a prominent location away from the main base. You can daub giant signs or mark the roads with spray paint. You can then hide and observe survivors as they gather at your collection point.

4 No matter how meagre your resources, all new survivors must go through the three stages of entry into the settlement. These are clearing, induction and integration.

5 Some groups will leave you no alternative but to fight. They will seek out your secure location and even assault it. Be ready for human opponents as well as dead ones and ensure that the whole team is ready to defend what you have. These groups will prey on the weak so hopefully overt displays of strength will deter them.

ZOMBIE HORDES

Where you come across a single zombie, it is always best to deal with them silently if possible. Avoid using firearms if you can as any noise will attract more of the walking dead. If you encounter a much larger group, known to survivalists as a 'horde' – then stop and move away as quietly as you can. Do not make any sudden dashes and keep your team in order. Be aware of wind direction as this may carry your scent. Never start a fight without very careful planning as you may find yourself facing more piling out from every side road or alley way.

WILD ANIMALS

Many beloved household pets will be left to fend for themselves in the aftermath of a major zombie outbreak. Now, you don't need to worry about roving gangs of hamsters but feral dogs will become more of a problem as time goes on. If you encounter a pack, never turn your back on it and slowly back away. Keep your weapon ready and if possible have some doggie treats in your kit bag which you can scatter liberally as you withdraw.

DEALING WITH THE CRAZIES

Weirdness will become the norm amongst the desperate and lonely survivors of the wasteland and for some; it will all be too much. Here are some basic guidelines for dealing with those who are rather rudely known as 'The Crazies':

▶ If you or any of your survivor group encounters a 24-carat mental case then the safest principle is to avoid where possible. You may encounter them briefly for the first time, keep any exchange to a minimum and from then on avoid 'mad town'.

▶ Where a crazy just sits watching you from a window or vantage point, avoid eye contact if you can. Do not look at them closely. They may just see you as potential raiders so move on and leave them in peace.

▶ If a crazy runs out in front of you and starts screaming about little people or any other such thing, you must remain calm. Use quiet and understanding language but keep one hand on your weapon. If possible, look for an opportunity to move on and leave the individual.

▶ Remember, the zombie apocalypse will put enormous pressure on people so don't blame them for cracking up. Where you can, you should try to support those in need. Time is a great healer – maybe they will change their 'crazy' ways and they might join your survivor group. You never know.

▶ DISGUISING YOURSELF AS A ZOMBIE

It is a common myth among many zombie survivalists that you can 'fool' zombies into ignoring you for an extended period by 'dressing up as a zombie'. This tactic has been successful in tests for very short periods of time, but the moment the survivor starts to sweat or gets too close to one of the dead, the zombie will 'clock' the human. It is a dangerous tactic to use but one which can be relied upon for a few minutes of respite in an emergency.

▶ Emit a low moan or growl but don't overdo it – this isn't drama school. It doesn't need to be continuous, get a feel for the vibe in your zombie group. If they are silent, you stay silent.

▶ Adopt a tired vacant 'student' look, with your head tilted to one side. Wearing a hooded top covered in blood can really add to the whole effect.

▶ Hang body parts such as intestines around your waist as a belt. Accessorise with other random internal organs in pockets. Ensure that all body parts are rotting.

▶ Wear a torn check shirt and ensure that it is covered in dried blood or at least red paint. Try to keep all flesh covered.

▶ Attempt a shuffling walk, possibly dragging one foot behind you. Again, don't overdo it and avoid the temptation to go faster than the rest of the horde.

▶ Keep your hair greasy and caked in mud or dirt. Add make up to really get that 'corpse look'.

▶ Drag a weapon along in your hand – it is important that you stay armed at all times. Zombies can often be seen dragging items so practise to make it look authentic.

▶ Avoid any close contact with the walking dead – even brushing alongside one of them could give you away if they catch the scent of a fresh human.

▶ Wear lots of deodorant if the weather is hot to help mask the scent of any sweating. And do not try to use this disguise if there is a chance of rain!

▶ Finally, avoid any other humans. It would be one hell of a way to go to survive the zombie apocalypse only to be killed by a fellow survivor who mistook you for a walking corpse!

> FEW PEOPLE LIKE BEING COVERED IN ROTTING HUMAN BODY PARTS. IF YOU FIND YOU ARE STARTING TO ENJOY THE EXPERIENCE THEN STOP DOING IT, OR PREPARE TO JOIN THE CRAZY CREW '

OUT AND ABOUT IN ZOMBIE TOWN

DRIVING IN ZOMBIE TOWN

Most survivors will have access to a motor vehicle of some sort, be it a fully-equipped, post-apocalyptic-ready Hummer or simply a motorised scooter. You should allow at least four to eight weeks before venturing far from your primary survival site. This will give time for the initial chaos to die down. However, even then, driving in a post-apocalyptic landscape will be fraught with danger and unseen hazards, and that's not even counting the flesh munchers lurking round every corner.

THE DANGEROUS TERRITORY OF A ROBBER BARON

A CRAZY LONE SNIPER WAITING FOR A TARGET

GANG OF BANDITS

FLOODED RIVER

RUBBLE AND OTHER DEBRIS IN THE ROAD

ZOMBIES CAUSING OBSTRUCTIONS

A SURVIVOR CONVOY KEEPING TO LOW SPEED WITH GUARDS

ROADS BLOCKED WITH BURNING CARS

THE HAZARDS OF DRIVING IN ZOMBIE TOWN!

ZOMBIES TRAPPED IN BUILDINGS

SMOKE FROM BURNING BUILDING OBSCURING THE ROAD

AUTOMOBILE TIPS

▶ Maintenance of your vehicle is essential – you do not want to either break down or run out of fuel with a few hundred ghouls watching you.

▶ Keep below 40mph. Most accidents will occur at speeds above this so keep the speed down unless it's an emergency. Many roads will have become blocked so expect obstructions.

▶ Know the capability of your vehicle and adjust your driving style accordingly. Don't try taking your modern hybrid through a deep ford only to get yourself stuck in mid-river, with salivating zombies on each bank.

▶ Get in a regular routine of pre-drive checks – tyres, battery, fuel and kit. Do these checks every time before you leave. Don't get caught out.

▶ If possible, go for a pre-1981 pickup in well-maintained condition. There is less technology on these older vehicles and you can still reasonably be expected to service them yourself. Get the latest four-wheel drive with onboard computer and you could find yourself stumped.

▶ Rotate your fuel supplies and add dates to cans so you can monitor usage.

▶ As a general rule, do not try to store more than 50 litres of flammable liquid in a residential location without some serious specialist storage facilities.

REMEMBER
F.I.T.B.O.W.

FLUIDS	Check your coolant and brake fluid levels and most importantly your washer fluid should be full as you will need to wash away blood smears.
INTERIOR	Check any Bug-Out supplies and you've got what you need for the mission.
TYRES	Inflated and carry a spare.
BASHERS	Onboard weapons for bashing.
OIL	Routine change and top up.
WINDOWS	Clear, with steel mesh secured in place.

⚠ REMEMBER

IF YOU ARE KEEPING A VEHICLE, YOU WON'T BE ABLE TO POP DOWN THE LOCAL GARAGE FOR REPAIRS. YOU WILL NEED A WELL-EQUIPPED WORKSHOP, WITH THE SUPPLIES AND SKILLS TO MAINTAIN YOUR TRANSPORTATION. *

Along with the correct Haynes Car Manual.

 MINISTRY OF ZOMBIES

▶ THE PERFECT ANTI-ZOMBIE VEHICLE

THE ZOMBIE KILLER

In 2010, a member of the Jordanian Royal family with strong links to the anti-zombie community offered a prize via his foundation to any engineer to come up with 'the perfect anti-zombie vehicle'. The rules called for the creation of a main vehicle, which should have the capacity to transport a group of survivors and be fit for general purpose use, and a smaller vehicle suitable for scouting or small-scale foraging. With the prize-money on offer, several major manufacturers entered and the winning designs, known as the 'Zombie Killer range' were announced in Amman in 2011.

Few survivors will have the time or resources to commission the building of one of these vehicles, but they are useful as you can take the ideas and implement them on your own vehicle. Think of these designs as the prototypes. Exciting developments such as the zombie scoop and firing platforms may be adapted onto your vehicle.

1 CHASSIS

Steel bar cage surrounding a padded cockpit for 4–5 fighters and supplies.

2 METAL BODY SCOOP

An adapted snow plough is welded to the front of the vehicle to push any run-down zombies up and to the sides of the vehicle.

3 SWIVEL MACHINE GUN TURRET

From this vantage point, a crew member can provide cover to any foraging teams or support by laying down fire into any hordes.

4 MOBILE MINI MORTARS

Smoke and sweat bombs may be fired at various angles from these small launchers.

5 TOUGHENED GLASS

The windscreen and side windows are special shatter-proof glass with optional darkening tint.

6 ESCAPE HATCH

Each model has an under vehicle escape hatch which can be used in emergencies.

7 LEG SLICERS

Each wheel is armed with extending metal blades which can be used to slice through zombie hordes.

8 EASY ACCESS

Two strong doors on each side so that an assault team can exit the vehicle swiftly and silently when on a mission.

9 STOWAGE AREA

Behind the seats there is an area for the stowage of weapons and foraged goods.

10 LIGHTING ARRAY

The vehicle is equipped with over 20 powerful lights, many of which can be directed from within the cabin.

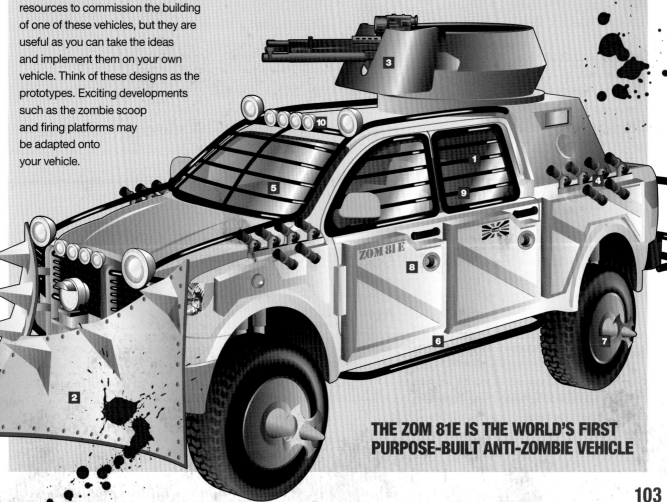

ZOM 81E

THE ZOM 81E IS THE WORLD'S FIRST PURPOSE-BUILT ANTI-ZOMBIE VEHICLE

OUT AND ABOUT IN ZOMBIE TOWN

LONG-DISTANCE TRAVEL

Mass air travel will be one of the first casualties of the zombie outbreak. As countries rush to quarantine themselves and skilled pilots and mechanics scatter, it is unlikely that many will get off the ground in the months that follow. The military can be expected to keep flying for longer, but air travel on civilian jets, small private planes and most helicopters has a definite shelf life.

The hero of post-apocalyptic air travel will be the humble microlite. Flying high above the grabbing hands of the dead is a tempting prospect against the alternative of making your way through bumper-to-bumper cars, blocked roads and zombie-infested towns and for sure some survivors will make their escape in various light aircraft and helicopters. But, being realistic, microlites certainly won't be available for everyone and if you live in an urban area then car travel alone is going to be a challenge. Most short-range missions will be on foot – this will include any local foraging or scouting patrols. Cycles can be a useful option, but motorcycles tend to be too noisy – what you get in speed is often negated when the sound attracts all of the walking dead within miles of your location. However, long-distance travel, say 20 miles or more will require much more planning and organisation. And, believe it, that 20 miles through a zombie-infested land will be a considerable challenge.

▶ LONG-DISTANCE TRAVEL THROUGH ZOMBIE-INFESTED AREAS

Longer journeys across zombie-infested areas, either on foot or in motorised transport, require skill and planning. Some journeys, such as a relocation to a more suitable long-term location, may be well-organised and structured while others, say following the collapse of your perimeter, may be more rushed and urgent. In the latter case, all survivors should make for one of the agreed Bug-Out locations, with their emergency supplies. **Do not be tempted to take any more – for now, survival is the key. If your perimeter has fallen, don't be tempted to start packing up supplies – if it's chaos then just grab your Bug-Out Bag and go.**

STEP 1
SCOUTING PARTY

Once the decision to move is made, use scouts to mark possible safe routes with spray paint and confirm the destination. Often working alone – these solo fighters may be able to secure sites en route for possible stops as well as checking the target location for zombies. Scouts should be light, fast and able to move quietly without attracting the attention of the dead. Typically, scouts should be fit and any experience in the armed forces is an advantage.

STEP 2
PACKING

Packing up supplies should be done in order of priority and according to how much you can reasonably carry. Allocate loads to different survivors and remember that your guards will need to be mobile so not everyone will be available for such duties. Never overload people and never slow down your guards. Budget for not more than 25 miles per day if you are on foot but this figure will vary greatly according to the level of fitness within the group. The golden rule is never to overburden the convoy.

OUT AND ABOUT IN ZOMBIE TOWN
RIVERS AND WATERWAYS

Foraging by boat can be an invaluable way to safely explore new areas or secure those supplies, but although zombies can't technically swim, they can still represent a danger in the water. Millions will become infected in the zombie apocalypse and many rivers and waterways will become clogged with the undead debris of grabbing ghouls.

ZOMBIE-PROOF FLOATING PLATFORM

Some zombie survival experts argue that the benefits of living afloat are such that it is worth investing your resources in developing a floating refuge. In essence, it's a large raft that could be tethered in a lake or wide river and from which you could operate, using smaller boats to make foraging raids on the shore.

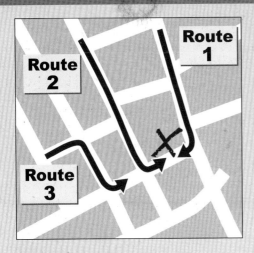

STEP 3
PLAN

Plan your main route carefully and have back-up routes in case you run into hordes of the dead. This is not a fighting mission – the objective is to reach the target destination with your survivors and supplies intact. Remember to budget to the speed of your slowest-moving vehicle or person. Ensure that you have temporary camping locations earmarked – this could be anything from an intact house to a tall tower where you can all huddle in safety on the roof.

STEP 4
PATHFINDERS

Use 'pathfinders' to track ahead of the main group. They will act as close scouts and check that routes are clear for slower vehicles. They will also monitor for any ambushes. During the actual move, keep guards on the flanks of the convoy. Try to keep a steady pace and do not stop to engage the dead unless you have to. Use a powerful rear guard, which can leave homemade bombs behind to deal with any 'tail of zombies' you might pick up.

During your convoy move, or any operation outside of your fortified base, it may be useful to use decoy techniques to draw the zombies away from your route of travel. Any noise or human commotion will attract the dead so sound can be a good decoy, but as zombies primarily hunt by scent, this can also be invaluable in sending the horde in the wrong direction by distracting them with bottles of sweat – though, of course, this scent must outweigh the amount being generated by your convoy as it struggles forward! It is most practical to keep the sweat in small grenade-like bottles.

SURVIVING THE APOCALYPSE

The 90-Day Survival Plan is just that – it's designed to get you through the first months of the crisis. However, once you reach Day 50 of the zombie apocalypse, you will need to turn your attention to linking up with other survivors.

It's not just about surviving; you need to take charge and build a survivor community capable of defending itself against any bandit groups as well as the walking dead.

Your first steps may be to send a lone scout to the immediate surrounding areas. Who has survived? Can you work together? Maybe you have friends in the local area? To survive in the long term, your group must expand, but it will always be a judgment call on who you can trust.

As a general rule, by Day 50 you should consider linking up with other survivors. The initial chaos will have died down, with maybe just hardcore looters

and a few surviving human groups out there. Expect to see zombies on every street, wandering aimlessly as their primary food source becomes more scarce. You can start small in the beginning but you should be planning for a few months down the line and establishing a major survivor colony.

The ideal set-up is to link with families and other survivors in your street or local area. You should establish yourself as leader. The expert knowledge you have picked up from this manual will help reinforce you as the obvious choice. You know what's happened, how it happened and what's going to happen next!

▶ A SURVIVOR CAMP – DAY 100

If your community has just settled in a suburban location then linking up a street or cul-de-sac may be the easiest way to provide a secure location. Other examples could include a large tower block or city block. There may be occasions when your current set-up is just not suitable for longer-term settlement. It will be dangerous transiting through zombie-infested areas, but some options and guidelines will be reviewed later.

1 Armed guards patrol keep points and the perimeter at all times. They work in 4-hour shifts and are looking out for both zombie and human threats.

2 The main entrance is blocked with two large buses, each with extra metal mesh welded onto the sides. They are simply reversed to open the route in for vehicles.

3 Regular patrols are out checking on the local area, looking for survivors and foraging for supplies. It's a dangerous job and these teams will soon become battle hardened.

4 A main residential block has been cleared and made secure for survivors. For the moment, everyone sleeps in the same block for security reasons.

5 An area for official notices and a notice board in which survivors can look out for anyone they know. Jobs and missions are also advertised here.

6 This secure area is known as the green zone and includes a small garden for survivors to enjoy. People need some escape from the constant tension and threats.

7 The whole perimeter of this small area has been checked and sealed. The survivors have used several buildings and a central courtyard to create a much bigger survivor settlement.

8 New survivors are still being found and go through a structured induction into camp life. Everyone has a role and everyone is expected to contribute.

9 A field canteen provides hot and cold food 24 hours a day as fighters and camp workers often work shifts. This is where they can relax and catch up on camp gossip.

10 A fortified command bunker from where the camp leader can supervise a growing community.

11 Foraged supplies are documented and stored in these containers. For example, the survivors are already stockpiling jumpers and coats for the winter months.

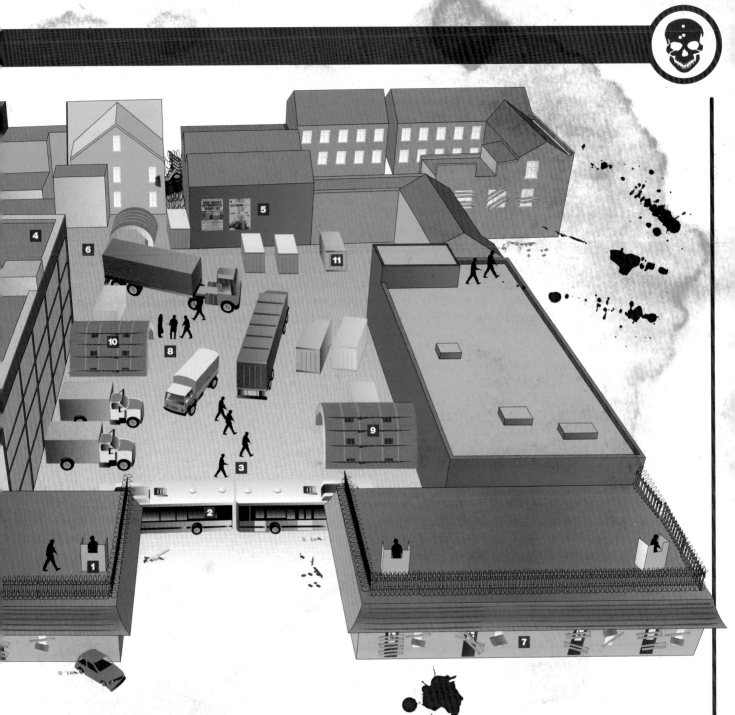

DEFENCE AND PERIMETER

Establish a defensive perimeter around your community. Clear the interior and then fortify. Use any existing barriers you can, for example, you can block the back of homes and use them as a wall.

FOOD AND WATER

You should gather all supplies together as soon as possible. Prevent individuals from hoarding food. You need to ascertain your current level of provision and create a communal food kitchen.

ALLOCATE ROLES

This can be ad-hoc at first but you will need a rota system for guard duty, kitchen duty etc. Audit the skills of your community and have crucial areas such as medical training covered.

POOL YOUR WEAPONS

You need to establish that you can defend your new community. Distribute weapons to your guards and create hand weapons for all survivors. Everyone should carry a weapon.

SCOUTS AND FORAGERS

Scouts should be sent out to map the local area and source for any urgent supplies. Your foraging teams should stay close and concentrate only on what your community needs.

ALWAYS LOOK TO EXPAND YOUR SETTLEMENT FURTHER BY SEARCHING FOR NEW SURVIVORS – HUMANITY WILL BE RELYING ON YOU – SO NO PRESSURE THEN!

SURVIVING THE APOCALYPSE

SURVIVOR INTEGRATION

Many of the survivors your scouts pick up will be shell-shocked, frightened and desperate. However, you should not simply introduce new members into your group without due process.

At the start, your integration process may be ad-hoc and consist of a brief medical check and a chat over a beer. However, as soon as you have the resources, you should structure the process to cope with increasing numbers of refugees in an organised way.

The Survivor Integration Model was designed by the Ministry of Zombies for just this purpose. It is a three-stage plan to incorporate people safely into your team. It is based on the core principle that these groups of individuals must be virus-free, safe to join your group and willing to sign up to your rules.

As leader, there will be some tough decisions ahead, one of which will be turning people away. What if they don't want to be part of your group? What if they look like 'trouble'? You will need to be a firm-but-fair leader. Making the hard choices comes with the territory.

SURVIVOR INTEGRATION MODEL	STAGE 1 CLEARING	STAGE 2 INDUCTION	STAGE 3 INTEGRATION
	Check that the new incumbents are virus free, and can safely be released into the community	Make clear the rules of the settlement and how to access essential services. Also, audit their skills	New survivors are allocated roles within the community according to their abilities and offered a mentor

STAGE 1
CLEARING

This first stage of the Survivor Integration Model is the important one – it includes your initial contact with the newcomers and will set the tone for the whole process through to their becoming a fully fledged member of your community. Ideally, your initial contact point should be away or at least outside of your main site. In most cases, your teams will be bringing in survivors they have found while out on patrols. The people they find will be frightened and suspicious, so ensure that they know exactly what is going to happen. It may be useful to have some refreshments ready as they come in to the waiting area. The main objective of the Clearing stage is to process the newcomers through until they are ready to start their formal induction process. So this includes initial contact, first interview and then a period of 24–48 hours in isolation.

NEVER RUSH TO PROCESS NEW SURVIVORS – IT ONLY TAKES ONE INFECTED INDIVIDUAL TO DESTROY YOUR SURVIVOR SETTLEMENT!

CLEARING 1
ESCORT TO CLEARING

A group of new survivors is discovered and escorted into a clearing station. They are welcomed but kept under guard for the moment. Your teams should provide food, water and shelter if required. If some survivors are clearly ill-suited to your settlement then you should escort them away from the clearing station.

STAGE 2
INDUCTION

This stage is about ensuring they understand the rules of the settlement and are thoroughly briefed on any intelligence of the zombies, other survivor communities and foraging sites.

- ☑ **We, the survivors, do pledge ourselves to building a safe and fair community.**
- ☑ **We will welcome others where it is safe to do so and work together, sharing the load and duties.**
- ☑ **We are dedicated to defeating the zombie menace in all its forms.**
- ☑ **We will battle bandits and those opposed to the above with everything we have.**
- ☑ **We pledge to obey our community commander until the end of the zombie war. At this time, we will facilitate and support a return to democracy.**

By joining this community, you agree to abide by the charter of this settlement.

STAGE 3
INTEGRATION

Once survivors have signed up they can be integrated fully into the community. This will mean having work and tasks allocated to them according to their skills and abilities. The process needs to include showing new arrivals the essentials around the base. They should have quarters allocated, know what time they are due at the canteen and have any defensive duties assigned.

TYPICAL INTEGRATION DAY
1. Tour of the base perimeter.
2. Talk through the rules and regulations.
3. Allocation of quarters.
4. In-depth intelligence debrief.
5. In-depth skills audit.
6. Commander meeting.
7. Final ceremony.

SURVIVORS MUST SIGN UP OR MOVE ON!

CLEARING 2
INTERVIEW

They enter a sealed area of your settlement. They are checked over by a medic and interviewed. Importantly, survivors must never feel like they've been arrested. At any time, they must be free to walk out of the process. However, they should not be allowed within your bases without going through clearing.

CLEARING 3
ISOLATION

The zombie virus is hard to isolate in the blood so as a precaution survivors are put in isolation pens for 48 hours. It is vital that new survivors keep to the rules and regulations of the settlement. You should have an internal militia force to manage law and order as your base of operations grows.

SURVIVING THE APOCALYPSE

THE USEFUL ZOMBIE

It will come as no surprise to many that government and international organisations around the world have already spent millions on studies to find a use for the walking dead. The United Nations feasibility report 455/AA is one such document and has been widely leaked across the internet. One of its declared objectives was:

> **TO PROVIDE INSIGHT INTO THE POSSIBLE UTILITY WHICH CAN BE MADE OF THOSE SUFFERING FROM THE ZOMBIC CONDITION, TAKING INTO FULL ACCOUNT THEIR EXEMPTION FROM THE UNITED NATIONS DECLARATION OF HUMAN RIGHTS BY AMENDMENT 40122A TO THE AFOREMENTIONED DOCUMENT**

UNITED NATIONS DOCUMENT ON ZOMBIC USAGE 455/AA OCTOBER 2007

Riveting stuff eh? But in a nation dominated by the walking dead, are there ways in which we can harness the power of the zombie for the benefit of all survivors?

ZOMBIES AS FOOD – A WARNING FROM HISTORY

In the small village of Del Peiro in Southern Italy in 1864, one very troubled priest sought to fight off the famine blighting his congregation by 'harvesting' zombies.

Father Claudio Baldini went on to produce a twisted document known as the *Zombie Cookbook*. It detailed how the living could take choice cuts from the dead and, with the right preparation and seasoning, prepare a palatable food source. Fragments of the book are said to remain in the Vatican Library and several pages are available online. The official Ministry of Zombies line states that in no way are zombies safe to eat. No cuts from a ghoul may be prepared in any way that would make them safe.

There are plenty of animals and possibly even people who would be classed as carrion-eaters – that is, they feed on the corpses of the dead as their main source of energy. Vultures are some of the most famous examples in the bird kingdom, but many insects and animals rely on things such as 'road kill' to survive. Now, in a world dominated by zombies, food will become increasingly scarce. It is estimated that survivors will have enough canned and dried food for a few years, but after this and unless we start to grow and harvest crops again, food will become increasingly scarce. There have been episodes of using the walking dead as a potential source of food throughout history.

WARNING – DO NOT EAT ZOMBIES!

1 POWER GENERATION

Any zombie power-generation machine must take into account the fact that zombies generally require 'motivation' for them to move. This is most often the scent of human flesh or blood. This principle is employed in the simple zombie power-generation design shown here, which illustrates how, with even a limited set-up, you can generate electricity to support your community. You won't have enough power to turn the air-conditioning back on, but working with 16 zombies on 12-hour shifts you should be able to generate enough power for lighting and basic cooking.

2 ZOMBIES AS FUEL

Nothing burns as well as dried zombies so, providing there has been no heavy rain and you are in an area of low humidity, the option of burning zombies for either power generation, warmth or just for the fun of it is worth considering. In terms of power generation, you are looking mainly at fuelling steam-power generators – imagine where coal was once used, you now just chuck on another corpse. Burning corpses is of course good practice anyway to restrict the spread of pests and the virus itself.

3 ZOMBIES FOR TRANSPORT

Again using the principle of 'motivation', it is possible to utilise a team of zombies to pull a simple cart or wagon. However, before getting carried away, be mindful that this idea relies on a regular supply of fresh human flesh.

> ⚠ **NEVER RIDE A ZOMBIE**
>
> **YOU MAY BE ABLE TO REMOVE THEIR TEETH AND REDUCE THE RISK OF A BITE, BUT IN GENERAL NOTHING POSITIVE COMES FROM TRYING TO CLIMB ONTO A ZOMBIE AND RIDING OFF INTO THE SUNSET.**

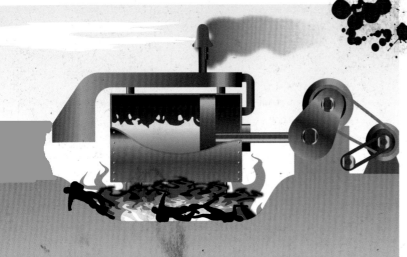

WORKING WITH THE DEAD

There are five key principles that all survivors should be aware of when working with zombies.

1 SNACK RADIUS

The first rule of working with the dead is that zombies will always reach, grab and bite for the flesh of the living. Creatures may have been de-toothed and de-clawed but you should always be aware of a zombie's 'snack radius' – the range at which it can grab a human – and manage your own safety carefully. It doesn't need to be a bite that kills as an infected scratch can do just as much harm.

2 SAFE STORAGE

Zombies must be safely stored any time they are not in use. Basic requirements include a sealed cage, preferably with a door that opens inwards. Any cage should be well maintained and bars are discouraged as the dead can easily reach through and grab one of the living. Storage areas should be well-lit, well-ventilated and, where possible, kept at a cool temperature.

3 COLLECTION TECHNIQUES

Always use approved techniques to restrain a zombie. An extended and locking neck-brace on the end of a pole is the best method. Such operations should never be attempted alone and it is recommended that each zombie is captured and then stored safely before efforts commence to secure another creature.

4 ZOMBIE BEHAVIOUR

Over several weeks in confinement, a zombie may appear to become 'dormant', particularly if it has little or no close contact with living humans. Be aware that a ghoul can snap out of this dormant state in seconds, becoming as dangerous as when it was first caught. Always 'wake' a zombie that appears to be in this state – normally, any noise or odour of the living will achieve this.

5 OTHER DISEASES

Cleanliness and personal hygiene cannot be over-emphasised when working with and handling the dead. Zombies are a veritable greenhouse for bacteria and infection, some of which are as dangerous as the zombie virus itself. Always wash and disinfect yourself after any contact with the dead and use protective clothing and eye wear at all times.

THE ZOMBIE CLEARING SYSTEM (ZCS)

The ZCS is a coordinated strategy for clearing an area, typically urban, which is infested with zombies. It was developed by the Ministry of Zombies in 2008, building on the new advances in zombiology and the experience of hundreds of zombie fighters. It is a system that can be used over and over again to transform a wasteland dominated by the dead into an area where frightened survivors can start to rebuild. Remember, not every battle in the zombie war will be a desperate last stand or a mass-zombie killing raid – you also need to think about gathering together survivors and developing your settlement into something that can support the real war against the dead.

HOW IT WORKS

The underlying principle of the ZCS is to isolate a substantial area, for example, several city blocks, by building a reasonable perimeter around the whole site. Your whole team will be involved in this task and should make use of any natural barriers such as rivers. You can also blow up buildings to block roads or seal houses to form a makeshift 'wall'. To complete the next phase of the system, divide your teams into three, each with their own roles: the Kill Squad to clear the sealed off area of the dead, the Clearing Squad to deal with any remaining ghouls, and the Rebuild Squad to make the environment habitable for survivors.

TEAM 1
THE KILL SQUAD KS
CLUBBING THE ZOMBIES ONE AT A TIME

Gung-ho zombie killers operating in squads of 4–5 fighters, these teams are sent in once an area has been sealed off. Generally, the squads work together for a general sweep of the main areas then split up for the nerve-wracking business of house-to-house zombie clearance. After clearing a building, they chalk or paint a large 'KS' on the door to show that it's been cleared. Kill Squad members must be tough, strong and experienced in zombie combat. They often see themselves as the elite of the zombie clearing system and you should develop cool team identities to help reinforce this.

TEAM 2
THE CLEARING SQUAD CS
FIGHTING THE DEAD WITH RUBBER GLOVES

Working in the Clearing Squad is no job for the faint-hearted. It's these survivors who clear the bodies from the streets and re-enter 'KS' buildings to clean up any blood splatter or remains. Once they've cleared a building, they add a 'CS' to the door to show it's been cleared for the next stage. Clearing Squad members must be able to handle themselves in combat as they will run into the odd zombie missed by the first sweep, but they also need a constitution of iron and the cleaning skills to match.

TEAM 3
THE REBUILD SQUAD RS
NAILING GHOULS TO THE FLOOR WITH DIY

The smallest team in terms of numbers, the Rebuild Squad follows on from the Clearing Squad and is responsible for ensuring that buildings are once again habitable for humans. They repair doors and generally zombie-proof the lower levels, turning each repaired home into a mini-bastion. They open up chimneys to create fire places and complete any insulation work required for a winter without heating. Once a building is fit for habitation, the squad adds an 'RS' to the door and may even add an 'H' if the dwelling is particularly habitable. Squad members are typically carpenters, plumbers and engineers.

SURVIVING THE APOCALYPSE

SURVIVOR GROUPS

Z-Day will change everything. The pillars of society will collapse along with any forces of central government, law and order. It is important to remember that as you develop your survivor community and start to take the war to the zombies, you will come into increasing contact with other survivor groups. Many will be 'normal' bands of survivors, only too willing to join your fight. Others will be far more dangerous.

As your scouts and foragers move further afield from your main settlement, you must ensure they have clear instructions on how to deal with the various groups and individuals they are likely to encounter. Be clear with them that the zombies are not the only threat out there.

A First-Contact Protocol has already been outlined (see page 100) for dealing with minor survivor groups and how to bring them into your community. Group First-Contact Protocols are more in-depth and include a range of responses based on the group you encounter.

Your teams should study the profiles of the groups and individuals they are likely to meet. There are several types of group that should be avoided at all costs unless you have the resources to engage in full conflict with them.

THE CITWR PROFILE

Using a team of post-apocalyptic experts from across the world, the Ministry of Zombies has developed the CITWR system to help your teams recognise and manage the most common groups of the wasteland.

CAPABILITY	The strength of the group, its numbers, set-up, resource level and military capability.
INTENT	The level of hostile intent towards either your community or activities in the zombie war.
THREAT LEVEL	The likelihood that this group will act with malcontent towards your community or the war effort.
WEAPONS	A measure of how dangerous and skilful the group is in terms of its firearms and other weapons such as blades and booby traps.
RESPONSE	Guidelines on how your forces should manage such a group and advice on any protocols for first contact.

 ### SURVIVING THE APOCALYPSE
PROFILE OF SURVIVORS

A Psychological Profile of Survivors after Day 120. This information was calculated using the FBI's complex modelling profiling system.

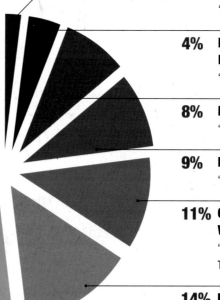

20% STILL HIDING
'Scared, so very scared!'

17% FIGHTING THE ZOMBIE WAR
'I'll die fighting for humanity if I have to!'

15% ORDINARY SURVIVORS
'A bit of foraging, a bit of hiding, always scared.'

2% DOING SICK THINGS
'I do bad things and I love it!'

4% PRETENDING TO BE ZOMBIES
'They accept me now.'

8% LONELY DRIFTERS
'I'm safer on my own.'

9% RELIGIOUS NUTS
'The Lord has cometh!'

11% CRAZY WASTELAND WARRIORS
'I ate cat yesterday. Tastes better than squirrel.'

14% LOVIN' IT
'I hated the old life anyway.'

 MINISTRY OF ZOMBIES

► SCAVENGERS OR LOOTERS

Numerous in the early months, some will take advantage of the end of the world to riot and grab what they can. Lacking the culture and infrastructure of an organised gang, some looters and petty thieves will join together as opportunistic and often violent looters – scouring the ruins for any survivors who can't defend themselves.

'GIVE ME ALL YOUR SUPPLIES OR I'M GONNA POP A CAP IN YOUR ASS!'

CAPABILITY
Most looters and thieves will be eaten or killed within the first month of the crisis. Opportunistic and ill-prepared, many will be caught in the open stealing items such as TVs and laptops – goods useful to them. However, a few will band together in groups of up to 30. They will work together to 'do over' survivor houses and look to survive themselves through looting and theft.

INTENT
Survival is their number-one priority. They will not want to see any return to law and order and will resist it but lack the capability for any sustained conflict. You may even find them offering to 'sell' your settlement their ill-gotten gains. Be aware, this won't just be foraged goods, this will be supplies taken from other survivors!

THREAT LEVEL
Thieves and looters are reluctant to engage in outright conflict with another organised group. Their profile is to pick on weaker targets. However, they can be dangerous when cornered and will be armed.

WEAPONS
Handguns held sideways are the weapon of choice for most urban groups whilst rogue grandma will be armed with anything from a 19th-century musket to a pump-action shotgun.

RESPONSE
You must be firm with this group. Defend your own territory with force and make plain your warnings about their activities. They can be a useful source for supplies, but over the long term thieves and looters must be dealt with. Some group members will willingly join you in the zombie war.

► FAMILY SURVIVAL GROUPS

By far the most common organised groups, these will be hungry and desperate bands of 'normal' survivors eking out a living in the wasteland and just about holding it together.

'JUST TURN AROUND AND KEEP WALKING.'

'WE DON'T NEED NO HELP!'

'CAN WE JOIN YOU?'

CAPABILITY
This groups tend to be small, mostly fewer than 12, and based around an extended family. They may have added additional neighbours to the group over the months of struggle. Resource-wise they will be just hanging on and typically armed with a few firearms and hand weapons. The rural farming variant of this group will be hardier and more independent as they have a more secure food source.

INTENT
Like many in the wasteland, family survival groups just want to stay alive. They most likely have children or the elderly in their home base and are desperately trying to carry on despite the ravenous dead just outside their window. There will be very little hostility towards your patrols unless they think you are looters.

THREAT LEVEL
The only time one of these groups will attack is when they consider you an immediate threat. They will have been attacked before and may be over-anxious in opening fire at any strangers.

WEAPONS
They may be armed with a few guns, but they will be ruthless in defence of their family. Grandad may be a Vietnam veteran and is likely to opt for the dwarf axe he bought on the internet.

RESPONSE
You must communicate your intentions towards this group clearly. Once they realise you are an organised community, fighting back against the dead, most will happily join up. Some will take longer so be patient. Also be aware that these groups can bring numbers of dependents into your settlement.

SURVIVING THE APOCALYPSE

▶ INNER-CITY GANGS

These tightly organised criminal gangs dominate many urban locations across the world and the zombie apocalypse, or 'zompoc', will be the perfect opportunity for them to increase their 'hood'.

'THIS IS OUR HOOD SO GET OUT OF THE HOUSE.'

'THAT'S NOT VERY FRIENDLY, WE ONLY WANNA SHARE!'

CAPABILITY
Well-organised and bound together by strong oaths of family, loyalty and upbringing, these groups will be a powerful force long after other criminals have disappeared under a wave of zombies. Numbers can be anything up to 100 core members but expect them to recruit big time when the dead rise.

INTENT
After years struggling against society and the police, this will be the time for gangs to take what they want. Expansion will be on the agenda, as will defeating any close rival gangs.

THREAT LEVEL
Medium to High. Inner-city gangs will be well-armed and motivated. They could be powerful allies or deadly opponents. Where their agenda revolves around drugs and human trafficking, you will have little option but to fight against them.

WEAPONS
Many of these gangs were 'tooled up' before the zompoc and with ready access to firearms, you can expect them to be heavily armed by the time you encounter them. They may not be formally trained, but they will be equally deadly with hand weapons such as baseball bats.

RESPONSE
Always learn about a street gang before opening up an attack. Treat them with respect and find out what their agenda is. Many will be young people thrown together for survival in a location that was deadly enough before the zombies arrived. If you can talk them round they could prove to be very useful fighters.

▶ BARONS OF THE ZOMPOC

Powerful individuals who have taken full advantage of the end of civilisation to build their own feudal kingdoms. Sometimes a particularly powerful gang leader, politician or business executive, even a bank manager, can evolve into this fully post-apocalyptic role.

'JOIN US AND END THIS PATHETIC ZOMBIE WAR.'

'I COULD USE A FIGHTER LIKE YOU.'

CAPABILITY
Barons are well-armed and equipped, with a fortified base and a close cohort of henchmen and women. They rule their local area, taking what they want from any survivors and even enslaving them as serfs. Some organised crime groups have all the infrastructure to move into this category.

INTENT
Power is everything to a Baron of the Zompoc. They are ambitious individuals with one paranoid eye on preserving what they have and the other on expansion and growing their 'kingdom'.

THREAT LEVEL
High. Barons will see any rival power as a threat to their cruel reign of terror. They could be powerful allies in your fight against the zombies but are likely to be distrustful allies. Their agenda is self-serving in their quest for more power.

WEAPONS
This group typically has stocks of firearms from before the zompoc to support their criminal activities. They'll have the access and knowledge to use them. Favourite weapons include the handgun, flick knife and knuckle duster.

RESPONSE
It may be possible to reach an uneasy peace with a Baron, for example by agreeing 'spheres of influence'. However, this will not last. Do not allow this group to infiltrate your settlement and in any direct conflict, go for the Baron and his or her loyal cadre. Take out these individuals and the clan will fall.

RELIGIOUS FANATICS

The end of the world will see the emergence of a whole spectrum of cults and religious groups. Many will be dedicated to fighting the zombie menace, fortified by their faith, and these groups can easily integrate into your operation. However, others will have a more sinister and downright evil agenda.

'HOW DO I KNOW WHAT GOD WANTS? HE TOLD ME.'

CAPABILITY

Cults are typically centred around one charismatic leader. Expect numbers to be anything from a small group up to 30 or 40. They will be totally dedicated, often sporting a vacant look and talking about 'the way'.

INTENT

This will vary from bringing about the end of mankind to growing a group for the self-interested if not self-appointed leader. Any interference with their group will lead to serious conflict. In some battles, their fighters will be fanatical, only stopped by death.

THREAT LEVEL

Medium. Approach these groups with caution. Carefully assess them and do not leap to conclusions based on their 'friendly' introduction. Learn about their religion and assess their weapons capability – some will be extremely well-armed.

WEAPONS

Many twisted post-apocalyptic cults will have the 'harvesting of the living' on the agenda and so a traditional scythe will be their favoured weapon. Expect the most organised cults to be well-equipped with other weapons and firearms.

RESPONSE

Always treat religious communities with respect, but where they are obvious cults, be tactful and cautious. Do not go to war without good reason and target the leader if possible.

CANNIBALS

With food scarce, some survivor groups will descend into cannibalism. Generally, this is a one-way street and once they have a taste for human flesh, they will rapidly descend into a group that regularly preys on other survivors.

'ONCE YOU'VE TRIED IT, YOU'LL NEVER GO BACK.'

'YOU LOOK SO HEALTHY AND WELL. DO YOU HAVE MANY FAT PEOPLE AT YOUR CAMP?'

CAPABILITY

These groups tend to be small, extended family operations in which members are closely bound together in their debauched lifestyles. All social norms will have broken down once the cannibalism taboo is shattered.

INTENT

Cannibal groups have no ambitions to take over. Their battle is to secure sources of human flesh. With this in mind, you will rarely come into conflict with them unless they are taking your people.

THREAT LEVEL

Low to Medium. The main impact of allowing a cannibal group to continue unhindered will be on the morale of the settlement. Knowing that the zombies are out there waiting is bad enough without the addition of devious humans as well. Cannibal groups cannot be allowed to survive in the medium term and fighting them will often mean wiping them out.

WEAPONS

The weapon of choice for cannibals will be the trusty meat cleaver. Sharp and with enough power to take an arm off in one swipe. Don't get too close.

RESPONSE

Groups will not declare themselves as cannibals on first contact. Ensure your teams can spot the warning signs such as human bones scattered around within their complex and any human adornments they may be wearing. Be prepared to use force as these fanatics will not be able to integrate back into 'normal' society.

SURVIVING THE APOCALYPSE

▶ EX-MILITARY AND ROBOCOPS

There is no question that our armed forces will put up a fight after the dead rise, but the sheer number of walking corpses will doom them to defeat. With this disintegration of command and control, various armed units will be left, without orders. Many will organise, using their experience in the forces to create a new group.

'I AM THE LAW! RESPECT MY AUTHORITY.'

'I AM REQUISITIONING YOUR SUPPLIES!'

CAPABILITY

These groups tend to have a hierarchical structure, with a former leader allocated the role of 'Commander'. Numbering anything from a small patrol to a battalion, these well-armed and trained groups will be in a strong position to survive as society collapses.

INTENT

The intention of this survivor group varies wildly from wanting to bring all of those left alive under their 'safe' control to being especially eager to link with other organised groups. Basically, in the wrong hands, an ex-military group will become little better than a strict robber baron with an authoritarian tilt. They can be brutal, decisive and quick to act.

THREAT LEVEL

High. Any encounter with a member of this group will be potentially risky. They must therefore be considered highly dangerous and any contact must be tightly managed. Over time, more groups will be become dominated by power-hungry leaders so after a few months, most will be hostile.

WEAPONS

These forces will be well-equipped with military- and police-grade firearms and supplies. One of the few groups with heavy weapons and even armoured vehicles.

RESPONSE

One tactic to attempt with ex-military groups is to recast your group as the 'central command'. You in effect will take over as their commander. Depending on their current leader, this can be a risky strategy. Open conflict with this group is not recommended, but they can prove to be invaluable allies in the war against the walking dead.

▶ MUTANTS OF THE WASTELAND

The zombie virus is always mutating and adding the possibility of a nuclear strike to clear cities of the dead. Survivors could encounter any number of genetic and zombic mutations.

'I AM THE NEW INHERITOR OF THE WORLD.'

'SOMEONE PLEASE JUST KILL ME!'

'DID I SEE YOUR FIGHTER. NO, I DON'T THINK I DID.'

CAPABILITY

Mutations are likely to be one-offs. They may be dangerous in combat, particularly if they are human/zombie hybrids, with the ability to think but with all the trappings of the ghoul. Most will be sad specimens doomed to wander the wastelands scavenging for food.

INTENT

Survival is their aim. Most will cower in the shadows, keeping well away from your patrols. You may occasionally lose a fighter where they have been snatched for food, but on the whole, mutants will have no great designs on your settlement if they are left alone.

THREAT LEVEL

Low. They can be dangerous in unarmed combat and there is the threat that they could spread a mutated form of the zombie virus. Avoid any bites or stings from mutants.

WEAPONS

Mutants could have a whole arsenal of unnatural weaponry from poison stingers in their tail to sharp bong hooks on their tentacles. They won't normally use firearms.

RESPONSE

Do not actively search out this group. Where mutants become an issue, you may need to 'cleanse' the situation, but for the most part, as long as they are not too powerful, give them a wide berth and leave them in peace.

▶ WALKING-DEAD LOVERS (WDL)

Sick individuals who keep family members or other zombies at home, typically chained to the bed. Some can't let go, others have altogether more depraved activities in mind.

'IT'S NOT UNNATURAL, THEY WERE HUMANS.'

'THERE MIGHT BE A CURE OUT THERE.'

'MY MOTHER IS STILL IN THERE SOMEWHERE.'

CAPABILITY

More often than not, WDLs work alone so the only challenge will be if you are trying to break into their dwelling. They have very little offensive capability. They will have weapons they started with and possibly a few more which have been foraged. Generally, they won't leave the side of their 'loved ones'.

INTENT

All WDLs want is to be with the one they love. They have no intentions towards your group unless you try to take out the ghouls in their care.

THREAT LEVEL

Very low. This group will not bother your settlement as long as you do not disturb them. There is the additional side benefit that they will take out the odd zombie that catches their eye.

WEAPONS

Weapons for self-defence only. Grandad's old shotgun is most common. Another favourite is the sledge hammer. This group is also a fan of booby traps so if your forces storm their house, be wary of some deadly traps as well as some sick and disturbing sights.

RESPONSE

Your scouts may make first contact with this group, but it is prudent to keep your distance. If they offer to introduce you to the rest of their 'family', politely refuse.

▶ AMAZONS OF THE APOCALYPSE

In the carnage and chaos of the first few months, people will band together for mutual protection. Some women will see this as an opportunity to break free of the discrimination in society. Using their growing skills in the martial arts, you may see the emergence of groups of amazons of the wasteland.

'OMG, THIS IS JUST THE MOST BITCHY SURVIVOR GROUP EVER.'

CAPABILITY

Fiercely loyal to one another and tightly bound together in a 'sisterhood of survival', these women will be skilful fighters and may verge on Baron-of-Zompoc-like behaviour.

INTENT

This group will rarely be hostile for no reason. If they attack then it is likely that one of your patrols strayed into their 'territory'. The primary aim of this group is survival and possibly to liberate others suffering under, say, a local Baron of the Zompoc.

THREAT LEVEL

Medium. This group may have been drawn together for protection, but their offensive skills are very real. If you cross them, they will respond with fury and force. Typically, this group will argue amongst themselves a great deal and you may find it hard to clarify exactly who is in charge. However, they have all the skills to be a deadly opponent.

WEAPONS
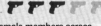

Archery clubs report over 51,000 new female members across America in 2012 so the weapon of choice will be the bow, backed up by firearms. Martial arts clubs added a further 110,000 new female participants in combat.

RESPONSE

Always send a female fighter as your first contact and approach them unarmed and with clear intentions. An Amazon group will never merge with your own immediately but you can build up a strong working partnership against the dead in battle. Plus, the Amazons will be very popular at social events.

▶ END-OF-THE-WORLD SCIENTISTS

With an ongoing mission to either kill mankind or cure the zombie virus, these isolated and lonely survivors could be either a curse or an invaluable ally in your battle with the dead.

'I JUST NEED MORE BODIES TO EXPERIMENT ON.'

'SOON ALL WILL KNOW MY NAME!'

'DO YOU HAVE ANY SPIDERMAN COMICS?'

CAPABILITY
Tending to work in total isolation, scientists working on the virus will be sealed away from the carnage in high-tech domes of safety. They may have one hard-pressed assistant, but other than that, they will be the sole survivors at their site. Their military capability is almost all defensive and may include automated defences such as turret machine guns.

INTENT
Most end-of-the-world types want to be left alone. Even if they are working to develop an airborne strain of the zombie virus, they will not be interested in minor groups of survivors. They have bigger things on their mind. If they are working on a cure, invariably nothing will be ready for testing.

THREAT LEVEL
Low. These research projects rarely come to anything. If left undisturbed, this group will happily work away in isolation. Even if they run out of supplies, they will not venture out, often preferring to take their own lives than face the dead.

WEAPONS
It's all about defence for this group. They will be safely sealed inside, defended by bulletproof glass and thick steel doors. The complex may be protected by automated defences.

RESPONSE
You won't find this group unless you go looking for it. The effort required to get into their 'lair' is often not worth it, with end-of-the-world scientists offering little more than vacant threats or promised deliverance. Best practice is to leave them alone.

▶ GENERATION Z

Very few family units will survive the zombie apocalypse intact and where children become orphaned or separated, they will herd together into gangs of youths known to zombie psychologists as Generation Z.

'OMG! I AM SO GONNA SKIN YOU ALIVE!'

'YOU WERE LIKE ON OUR PATCH LIKE. THERE'S NO WAY YOU CAN GET AWAY WITH IT. LIKE.'

CAPABILITY
These groups will tend to be up around 40 in size. Any larger and they tend to splinter. Based around teenagers, kids of various ages will group together, bound by a fierce sense of loyalty. Without any parental guidance or authority, they will be capable of great kindness and cruelty. They will be very able to defend themselves.

INTENT
Like many groups, survival is the name of the game. Depending on the leadership they may be aggressive towards outsiders and will have little interest in your zombie war from the start.

THREAT LEVEL
Low to Medium. The main flashpoint with Generation Z will be around foraging and supplies. If you don't enter their territory, you will be unlikely to come into direct contact with them. However, some of the children will grow up after Z-day, and this world will be all they've ever known. They will be tough, seasoned zombie fighters, more than capable of killing to survive.

WEAPONS
These kids will be experts in the use of the catapult for hunting and, make no mistake, it can also be a deadly weapon against human opponents. They are also likely to be skilled in firearms, copying the handgun held sideways stance of larger gangs.

RESPONSE
These feral children can be unpredictable and violent so a cautious and soft approach is required. Do not come across as the 'adult' or too heavy handed. Respect their boundaries and earn their appreciation. It will be a long and fraught process to bring Generation Z children into your settlement.

MAD LONERS

For some, the madness of the zombie apocalypse will be too much. Many mad loner and crazed survivors will have started out within a group, perhaps it was overrun and massacred. Now, their only agenda is chaos and ever-increasing levels of craziness.

'I'M NEVER ALONE WITH MY INVISIBLE FRIENDS.'

'THE VOICES KEEP SPEAKING TO ME. THEY ARE TELLING ME TO LIGHT FIRES!'

CAPABILITY

One individual can do a lot of damage and you can expect these individual activities to range from running around naked dodging the zombies to lighting fires and screaming that they are going to 'burn everything away'. This profile always operates alone.

INTENT

The response of these individuals to outsiders varies greatly. Many will simply hide and come out only when you are gone. Others will sneakily follow your patrols back to base and then spy on your activities. Most will just want to be left alone.

THREAT LEVEL

Medium. The level of insanity with these individuals ranges from slightly crazed to homicidal maniac. The most dangerous individuals may embark on a killing spree or attack your patrols, but the most likely threat is their habit of starting fires. If one of these uncontrolled blazes reaches your survival settlement, things could get very ugly, very quickly.

WEAPONS

Fire is the mad loner's best friend and greatest weapon. They will be armed with other firearms and weapons, but they have a habit of starting blazes with cans of petrol where they can do most damage.

RESPONSE

If you have an experienced counsellor, you may be able to talk these characters around, but it is unlikely. The particularly violent ones can do a significant amount of damage in which case decisive action will be required.

WASTELAND WARRIORS

For some men and women, the death and carnage of the zombie apocalypse will be an awful liberation. The pillars and constraints of society will be gone and they wander the ruins of civilisations looking tough and offering rock-hard one liners.

'I USED TO WORK IN A CALL CENTRE.'

'I DON'T WANT ANY TROUBLE, I'M JUST LOOKING FOR MY SON.'

CAPABILITY

Warriors of the wasteland typically survive alone. Sometimes there are two but never more than this. They will be carrying what they need to survive, living day-by-day and foraging where they can. They will be well-armed and skilled with their weapons. At the start there may be many of these types, but only the best will survive as the months progress.

INTENT

Generally, warriors are good guys or girls. They are often driven on by the loss of their family or maybe even in search of them. Their old lives are in ruins and the zompoc has transformed them. They are well-adapted to survive in zombie-infested areas.

THREAT LEVEL

Low. This group will rarely threaten your survivor community unless they are attacked first. Also, do not try to restrict these individuals from travelling through your 'territory'. They are usually loners and will only forage what they need.

WEAPONS

Warriors of the wasteland will have every type of weapon in that backpack, from shotgun to handgun, machete to samurai sword.

RESPONSE

Be firm but friendly towards these warriors. They could be powerful allies in the war against the zombies. Respect their freedom to roam and offer them smaller missions for payment to help bring them into your fold. Offering to replenish their supplies and ammunition will be well-received and help you to build a relationship.

ZOMBIE SURVIVAL EXAM

ZOMBIE SURVIVAL BASIC LEVEL

This paper has been approved by the Ministry of Zombies in London and the State Department for Defense against the Walking Dead in Washington DC. Citizens are encouraged to undertake this examination and are awarded a Basic Level in Zombie Survival upon successful completion.

INSTRUCTIONS TO CANDIDATE

▶ You should attempt all questions on the paper.
▶ You must base your answers on the content of this manual.
▶ Don't go making shit up.
▶ For the 20 questions, you should score 15 or above to pass.
▶ 10 minutes. This is a closed-book examination.

1 Which of the following are warning signs of the zombie apocalypse?
- **A** The media is full of reports of 'unexplained cannibalism'.
- **B** My supermarket has a two-for-one offer on avocados.
- **C** Re-runs of *Dawn of the Dead* on television.
- **D** You had a nightmare about zombies.
- *i* **p24**

2 How do you 'kill' a zombie?
- **A** Threaten it verbally.
- **B** Chase it away and it will die of hunger.
- **C** A stake through the heart.
- **D** Smash at least 80% of the brain.
- *i* **p10**

3 Which of the following causes the development of the zombic condition?
- **A** Voodoo.
- **B** Being in a cemetery at night.
- **C** The zombie RNA virus.
- **D** Radiation.
- *i* **p13**

4 One of the most important features of zombie home defence is:
- **A** A nice glass conservatory.
- **B** A white picket fence.
- **C** A landscaped garden with delightful water feature.
- **D** Double- or triple-glazing on all windows and doors.
- *i* **p40**

5 Which of the following is a good zombie survival location?
- **A** A hospital – they're bound to have a cure.
- **B** A Church – it's bound to be safe there.
- **C** A big tent in the middle of the park.
- **D** A fortified and fully supplied home.
- *i* **p56**

6 Which of the following is a component of any Bug-Out Bag?
- **A** Essential food and water for 24 hours.
- **B** The latest copy of *Vogue*.
- **C** A TV Guide.
- **D** Your priceless collection of *Star Trek* figurines.
- *i* **p30**

7 Your granny has been bitten by a zombie. What do you do?
- **A** Forget about it, it's only a scratch.
- **B** Get her started on some antibiotics.
- **C** Give her a stiff drink and quietly get the hammer.
- **D** Try to cleanse and bind the wound.
- *i* **p11**

8 Which of the following is a better weapon to fight zombies with?
- **A** An empty gun – it might scare them off.
- **B** A metal baseball bat – ideal for bashing brains.
- **C** A rapier sword – for striking with precision at the heart.
- **D** A small fruit peeler from IKEA.
- *i* **p65**

9 Which scientist is known as the 'father' of zombiology?
- **A** Dr Khalid Ahmed.
- **B** Dr Spock.
- **C** Dr Beverly Crusher.
- **D** Dr No.
- *i* **p22**

10 Why should you watch plenty of approved zombie films?
- **A** Because they are a great substitute for any real training.
- **B** Because I believe everything on TV.
- **C** Because they may present some realistic survival scenarios to learn from.
- **D** I don't have anything else to do.
- *i* **p26**

11 Do you believe that zombies should have human rights?
- **A** Of course, they're people too.
- **B** No way. It's kill or be killed.
- **C** We should offer them something.
- **D** Sure, why not? Maybe we could all live together.
- *i* **p22**

12 Your attitude to zombie survival can best be summed up by the following statement:
- **A** No, no, no – they don't exist!
- **B** I plan to join Team Edward.
- **C** I want to join the undead horde, it sounds like a laugh.
- **D** I'm trained, I'm prepared and I'm going to survive.
- *i* **p26**

13 Which of the following is not a type of zombie?

A A classic.

B A limbless wonder.

C A double zinger with cheese.

D A snapper.

i p92

14 Which of the following is a recognised post-apocalyptic survival group?

A Barons of the Zompoc.

B Door-to-door sales people.

C The Moonies.

D Cancelled cowboy space series fans who complain endlessly.

i p114

15 Putting zombie warning posters up around my neighbourhood will:

A Tell people I'm mental.

B Encourage children to chase and throw stones at me.

C Warn people about the very real threat they face.

D Give me something to do.

i p36

16 You come across another survivor group when out foraging, do you?

A Run and hug them.

B Kill them all and run away screaming.

C Entice the zombies towards them.

D Treat them with caution, being firm but friendly until you know their motives.

i p100

17 Which of the following is not a symptom of the zombic condition?

A A slow stumbling walk.

B A desire to feast on human flesh.

C Fangs.

D A vacant gaze and no speech.

i p6

18 I would describe myself as a 'zombie survivalist' by saying:

A I mean the zombie books are okay, but vampires are cooler.

B Not really. I enjoy the films enough.

C Yeah – as a joke. They're fictional anyway.

D I would proudly describe myself as a zombie survivalist and go to explain the dangers of the walking dead to others.

i p26

19 You can safely eat zombie meat as a healthy alternative to beef:

A Indeed. It's is particularly nice with a fine mushroom sauce and sipping a good Chianti.

B You should never eat zombies – it's foul and may spread the infection.

C Why not, I'll try anything once.

D This makes sense as fresh meat will be hard to get.

i p110

20 Does the average person need to do any special preparation for the zombie apocalypse?

A No – it's best to just take it as it comes.

B No – I plan to go *Mad Max* anyway.

C Yes – I bought a lovely new set of camouflage trousers.

D Yes – people need to embark on a complete programme of zombie survival preparation and training.

i p46

ANSWERS

20 D	19 B
18 D	17 C
16 D	15 C
14 A	13 C
12 D	11 B
10 C	9 A
8 B	7 C
6 A	5 D
4 D	3 C
2 D	1 A

YOUR SCORE • BASIC LEVEL

15-20 You have a good understanding of zombie apocalypse preparation and the threats these creatures face to humanity. You have achieved the level required and are awarded a Basic Certificate in Zombie Survival. Any score over 17 entitles you to a merit score.

10-14 You have clearly learnt lessons from this book, but you have not quite achieved the required standard. Check back through the chapters you did not understand and then sit through the paper again.

Below 9 This is below average and most unimpressive. One wonders if you are taking this whole zombie survival thing seriously. Either go back to the start of the book and start cramming or become a quick and easy snack for the dead when they arrive.

In 2009, the Ministry of Zombies consulted with several government bodies after being asked to review the possible development of zombie survival certification for both children and adults. The project was shelved in 2012 with ministers citing 'cost concerns' as the main reason. Here at the Ministry of Zombies, we still maintain that Tahiti was the best location to review and produce our research.

Only two sample papers were created and are presented here for the first time. After thoroughly reviewing the content in this book, you should attempt to complete Paper 1 to achieve a Basic Certificate in Zombie Survival. After further study and training, you should move on to Paper 2 to achieve an Advanced Certificate in Zombie Survival.

ZOMBIE SURVIVAL EXAM

ZOMBIE SURVIVAL
ADVANCED LEVEL

Do not attempt the Advanced Level paper until you have completed your Basic Level qualification. The Advanced Level Certification provides you with a survival profile – you must score in the top two boxes to pass and achieve certification.

1 **There is one course of action when a survivor has been infected:**

A Chop, chop and chop again with an axe.

B There is no cure so isolate them and consider the end game.

C Give them paracetamol – might be flu.

D Set them free to join the rest of the zombies.

2 **A group of survivors arrives and hammers on the door – they want to come in and escape from the zombies:**

A Tell them to get lost, you've got the supplies but you ain't one to share

B Find out more about them, then quarantine them and have them join your group.

C Open your door and give them the help they need.

D Run outside and hug them, it's been weeks since you've seen anyone.

3 **You look at your current home and decide to make some improvements. Do you?**

A Take out the stairs to provide a well-defended 'green zone' on the upper floors.

B Complete a Zombie House audit and act on the outcomes.

C Consider double-glazing but it is expensive.

D Put a delightful rockery in by the pond.

4 **You find an injured survivor along the road. He has clearly been bitten. Do you?**

A Put him out of his misery and steal all of his supplies. He won't be needing them soon.

B Knock him out when he's not looking and then take all his supplies.

C Allow him to travel with you until he turns.

D Sit down and talk about the old days.

5 **You are captured by a group of cannibals. Do you?**

A Offer to bring them more human survivors if they let you go, then honour this foul pledge.

B Fight to the death, hoping to clean the earth of this sickening scum.

C Call them inbred mutants and say you will be writing a letter of complaint.

D Try to talk them round to your vegan stance.

6 **You are out foraging and come face to face with another armed survivor – you are both looking at the same box of supplies. Do you?**

A Offer to share it, then throw sand in her face and make a run for it with the supplies.

B Make a genuine offer to share the booty.

C Offer her all the supplies and agree that she saw them first.

D Surrender with all your supplies.

7 **Zombies can be best described as:**

A Creatures which must be destroyed.

B Humans suffering from the zombic condition.

C The 'mortally challenged' – they're people too you know.

D Made-up creatures called Edward or Jacob.

8 **You encounter a group of UN soldiers. They say they are evacuating people, starting with the elderly. Do you?**

A Dress in a cardigan and limp through their checkpoint as if you are 80.

B Applaud their rescue attempt and help them to guard the complex.

C Offer to help in their medical tent.

D Agree to help search for elderly survivors.

9 **Which answer best summarises your approach to the zombie apocalypse:**

A I'm armed, trained and ready for it to kick off. In fact, I'm quite looking forward to it.

B I'm fearful. I've made some preparations, but my social life keeps getting in the way.

C I've bought all the books and plan to read them later.

D Zombies don't exist so it's not worth doing any planning.

10 **Your ideal role during the zombie apocalypse is:**

A A powerful baron of the zombie apocalypse, with hundreds of fighters at my disposal.

B A key member of the anti-zombie army, fighting to liberate the country.

C I want to use it as a chance to develop myself in so many areas.

D I want to join the undead and start sparkling in the sunshine.

11 **Your perfect weapon against the zombies is:**

A Anything that enables me to kill the most zombies or survivors if they get in my way.

B A trusty clubbing weapon, easy to carry and robust.

C I'd carry a long stick so I could poke the zombies away. I prefer not to kill.

D I never carry weapons, I'm a pacifist.

12 **What is the Zombie Clearing System?**

A A way to bash every undead zombie in an area.

B A strategy to clear zombies from an area.

C It's using trains to get rid of the dead.

D It's some kind of soap for cleaning the dead.